The
Parenting
Business

The Parenting Business

Hindsight is 20/20

Carolyn Esparza, MSW/LPC

Tsaba House
Reedley, California

Cover design by Mayapriya Long, Bookwrights Design
Typography by Pete Masterson, Aeonix Publishing Group
Senior Editor, Jodie Nazaroff
Cover photo by Andrea Schwagerl

All scripture quotations are taken from the *King James Version* of
the Bible.

Cataloging in Publication Data
(Provided by Quality Books, Inc.)

Esparza, Carolyn
     The parenting business : hindsight is 20/20 / Carolyn
Esparza. -- 1st ed.
     p. cm.
     Includes index.
     LCCN 2003110366
     ISBN 0-9725486-7-x

     1. Parenting--Religious aspects--Christianity.
     2. Parent and child--Religious aspects--Christianity.
     3. Problem children--Religious life. 4. Family--Religious
     life.   I. title

BV4529.E86 2004   248.8'45
                                   QB104-700061

First Edition: April 2004

Published by:
Tsaba House
2252 12th Street
Reedley, California 93654

Visit our website at: www.TsabaHouse.com
Printed in the United States of America

Dedicated To

The four greatest blessings in my life, my four children—without whom, I would never have known the blessing of parenthood; and to my own parents, Marvin and Charlotte Harrison.

With Deep Appreciation

Dale Andrews, Pastor
Dave Hendrickx, Pastor
Donna Durocher, Mother & Therapist
Jane Kruse, Mother, Encourager & Friend
Jesse Morales, Father & Pastor
Kathy Hendrickx, Mother & Teacher
Lorraine Herbel, Mother & Grandmother; raising a Grandchild
Margaret Brooks, Mother & Educator
All of those parents and children who have provided me with 20/20 hindsight, for your time, encouragement, honesty and suggestions.

Contents

In The End

Now when Solomon had made an end of praying, the fire came down from heaven, and consumed the burnt offering and the sacrifices; and the glory of the Lord filled the house.   *— 2 Chronicles 7:1*

For Mother's Day several years ago, my children gave me a computer. My oldest son builds computers, so his brother and sisters apparently pooled their money to help him build me a more modern computer than the one I had been plugging away on for years. They secretly set it up in a back bedroom and called me in, as if there were a pressing need. I walked into the room where they all were lined up together, with cameras flashing to catch my expression.

As an awareness of what they had done came over me, I was moved to tears. The tears had little to do with the computer, but everything to do with how they presented it to me. They planned it, *together*. They coordinated it, *together*. They set it up, *together*. They presented it to me, *together*. I love walking into the computer room and reading each of their names as they roll across the "Happy Mother's Day" screensaver: a reminder of their unity, a remembrance of the occasion we were all together as a family for—Mother's Day. Then, this past Mother's Day, I received the following letter:

Dear Mom,

Happy Mother's Day... I looked and looked for a gift for you... for some reason, I could not find the perfect gift. I am not sure why, but I kept thinking, this is really not about gifts at all. This should be about letting you know how very special a mother you are. My mind kept

11

going back to all of our stuff in the storage shed, stored away. Although it is nice to have nice things they are just things, and really have no value or meaning.

I guess what I am trying to say, is that I worked very hard this year not to buy you a fancy gift with a fancy card. I figured that your gift should be just telling you how I feel about having you as a mom. You have been very special to me over the years, and supportive. I want to thank you for that.

Thank you for raising us and being there when things were both good and bad—it takes a very special person to be there during the bad times. Thank you for building a good foundation of morals and work ethics.

Thank you for all the trips to the pool, museums, parks… for driving over the water at Brackenridge Park over and over and over again, for all the garage sales and flea markets, for watching us while you were trying to sell your art work downtown on the Riverwalk. All those things helped to build us into the people we are today.

Thank you for helping us to set our standards high and for helping us reach our goals with your love and support. Mom, you are "Simply the BEST." Have a wonderful day and Thanks for being my mom for the past 33 years.

Love, Kayla

Do I share this with you to brag about what a wonderful mother I've been? Of course I do! Unfortunately, you will soon learn that is *not* the truth.

The greater purpose in sharing this is to emphasize that what is important to our children has nothing to do with what we give them materially, and everything to do with what we give them spiritually. *In the end,* what is important to our children, is what they carry with them through life in their hearts. Even scientific surveys tell us children would much rather have their parents' *attention, affection, approval and acceptance* than any material item. As parents, why don't we get that?

It is with that thought I pray that your own challenges in parenting will be rewarded with the very BEST gift a parent can receive—the pronouncement of your own children that "You are the BEST," because you shared your time and your heart with them.

Acquiring
20/20 Hindsight

Receive my instruction, and not silver; and knowledge rather than choice gold. For wisdom is better than rubies; and all the things that may be desired are not to be compared to it.
— *Proverbs 8: 10-11*

How naïve I was when my first child was born. I armed myself with the current "parenting Bible" and several dozen diapers and was ready to parent. Neither the pregnancy nor my labor was difficult. Obviously, I must have been created for parenting!

The nurse whisked into my hospital room, all smiles. "Here's your beautiful little girl," she quipped as she plopped a pink bundle into my arms and vanished

"Stop! Where are the instructions?" I wanted to yell.

I propped the warm, pink bundle on my knees and stared at it. I can still see those defiant jet black eyes staring down a barely visible nose right back at me, as if it was this morning. It was a look that clearly said, "So, now what are you going to do with me?"

My heart skipped a beat, or maybe two. I had no earthly idea what I was going to do with her. Who was this little twerp, no more than six hours old, to be so all knowing? How did she already know that she had the upper hand? I felt totally inadequate to fill a role for which I had longed. Time proved me right.

Although at the time I had no measure for comparison, I now know Kayla was a remarkably pleasant baby. She did all she could to help me parent her. Kayla cried when she was hungry, burped when

I patted her back, squealed when she pooped, and the rest of the time, she sat calmly, staring at me knowingly.

When she was eighteen months old her brother, Brent, arrived. From the moment we brought him home there was nothing but wailing. Especially at night, he wailed away, furiously rocking himself to the top of his crib, incessantly banging his head against the headboard. Brent worked up such a steam, that the paint eventually melted off the headboard at the spot he continually banged, and he wore a perpetual coin sized bruise on his forehead.

You might ask, "Was something wrong with him?"

If there was something wrong, we never found out what it was despite a parade of physicians, psychiatrists and therapists probing all of us physically and mentally for years. We remained baffled by this child throughout the years. He was expelled from every school he attended, including pre-school and kindergarten. Ultimately, when he was sixteen, sitting in the principal's office after yet another incident, I informed him he was quitting school and getting a job because "I spend more time at this school than you do."

Melissa was born when Brent was almost two. A new baby, with two children in diapers—one of which was a super-distressing two-year-old—what were we thinking? I now had a comparison. This was a supremely good child. Melissa smiled from the minute she was born. She let her older brother and sister carry her around like a rag doll as they plopped her into the doll cradle their father built, and rocked her for hours. They made paper crowns to adorn her head, and insisted on photographing "the queen." They loaded her into the little red wagon and pulled her everywhere they went. Only twenty-five years later, did she report that her brother pushed her out of the twelve-foot tree house to the grass below. They conspired together never to tell, because we might take down the tree house. All that, and she never complained! It terrifies me to think of it, even today.

Joshua arrived when Melissa was just over two—another pleasant, smiling baby with an exceptionally high tolerance for sibling intervention. He evidenced his penchant for diplomacy at two months of age, when they shared chicken pox with him! Not a murmur of complaint! He was only two when his father and I divorced.

I knew for some time that the relationship had deteriorated. I must acknowledge that I was as much at fault as he was, if not more.

We were entering the age of "equality for women." I needed a purpose. I needed a career. I needed freedom. I needed, I needed, I needed!

Before we married, actually even before I attended college, I wanted to be a social worker. To this day, I don't remember where I had even heard of social workers. Nevertheless, the desire remained. Unfortunately, my mother had some archaic ideas about social workers and when I was applying for college, my parents informed me that they would not provide my college tuition if I intended to become a social worker.

At that time college was more an opportunity to leave home than an academic pursuit for me, therefore I opted to have my parents pay the tuition. I enrolled as an art major. After a few semesters I realized that art was my therapy, not my passion, and changed my major to English. Why that? My thinking at the time was that I wanted to stay away from home and I liked to read! It was with that type of logic that I pursued an education! Four years later, I graduated with a major in English and a minor in the closest thing I could come up with to defy my parents and fill my need—sociology.

The summer I graduated, I married. Through a college roommate I found a job as a legal secretary for a corporate attorney with reams of tedious, boring documents to type. However, in the same office was a criminal attorney. He was too frugal to hire his own secretary, so he paid a few dollars to various secretaries in the office to come in on Saturdays and type up his work. I loved the work and urged him to hire me full time, to no avail. However, I did become the primary "girl-Saturday" for about two years. Attempting to understand the psychology behind the crimes of the perpetrators he represented was intriguing to me. There was no way I could have known how well this experience would serve me in years to come.

I worked until a few days before my first child was born. It was just assumed that I would then stay home as a full time mom. I became involved in motherly things; I fed, diapered and potty trained. I became adept at making boo-boo's go away with a kiss and a Band-Aid. I packed up a car full of children and headed for the park. I planned birthday parties and baked birthday cakes. I helped at the nursery school, kindergarten, and first grade. I decorated the house and redecorated. I became involved in a woman's organization or two, and even got "hooked" on soap operas.

Nine years later I was bored, unfulfilled and searching. I made the decision to begin studying for my master's degree in social work. From the first course, I was enthralled. I also took a part time job, only nine hours a week, at a family service agency. I loved getting out of the house for what I believed to be a "real purpose." I was thrilled to be interacting with others having my same interests. I felt a semblance of fulfillment.

I asked for a divorce. He was not surprised. He moved out and, of course, the reality of divorce was as shocking as the reality of parenthood. I had no income other than nine hours a week at minimum wages; however, I was determined to be super-woman. I would raise these four children; continue my education and work. I could do it all. Whether I could remain sane doing it all never entered my mind!

I can't even remember the number of piecemeal jobs I put together to fend off creditors. I know there was the nine-hour a week job that eventually grew to twenty hours. I sold Tupperware, drove a woman to and from work for gas money, and put together a children's art class in my home.

The day came when I was a full-fledged master's level social worker. By then, I had lost a custody battle for my children. They were now living 150 miles away and visiting me on weekends. I had also undergone chemotherapy, radiation and all that goes with cancer. It was "the best of times and the worst of times." The pain of "losing" the children went beyond excruciating. The fear of having cancer was my salvation.

My professional life was satisfying; it led me from the family service agency to rewarding years of work in the area of adoption. Adoption led me right down the road to prison. My work with juvenile offenders remains the highlight of my direct service experience as a social worker. Ultimately, I moved into administration and found I truly enjoyed sharing my experience with others. Mentoring newcomers to the field was certainly fulfilling.

Over the years, one by one, my three oldest children returned to live with me. The youngest remained with his father. Years later I learned that was not only an agonizing void in my life, but in his as well. Over the years anger gave way to understanding and healing; I learned that what starts out on rough footing, can become some of the most holy terrain in life.

Navigating the teen years with my children was more than challenging. This was especially so, because of the disruption of the divorce and the custody matters. That was compounded by the fact that I had not yet found the fulfillment I was still seeking. That was still to come.

It is because of this struggle and because we endured it, that some thirty-three years later, we are a family—not a perfect family, but a supportive, loving family, that I share our story. Because I know that knowledge is power, I share the proceeds of the 20/20 hindsight, which I've gained from my years in the parenting business, both personally and professionally. I do it with the profound hope of helping others wrestling with the demons that seem inherent in raising children, to know that without a doubt, there is hope.

Family Unity
In Cyber-Space

Better is an handful with quietness, than both the hands
full with travail and vexation of spirit. — *Ecclesiastes 4:6*

There is a real trick to building and maintaining working relationships with children. Unfortunately, in our quest to build a faster world, the magic to execute that trick was lost. The magic we lost was "work." Working relationships require "work."

That was a shock! Growing up in "Leave It To Beaver"–"Father Knows Best" days, I assumed all family problems—if there were any—were resolved in thirty minutes amidst laughter and hugs, with time out for commercial breaks.

Now, after biting the bullet of reality for well over thirty years, I know all working relationships require at least as much work from one member of the relationship, as they do from the other. Before we enter a relationship, especially a relationship with children, it behooves us to make a commitment to **work** on that relationship. Children must be taught how to have and hold a relationship, before they can enter the relationship workforce. That requires at least triple-duty from the parents. Parents must be teachers and role models, as well as active participants in the relationship with their children. None of these roles is easy.

In our ultra-busy society, we have become hooked on a fast food life-style. As the economy has changed over the decades, we have seen the family emerge from a "gather-'round-the-table-and-say-our-prayers-and-have-a-warm-and-animated-discussion-family-unit" to "grab-what-you-can-catch-if-you-can-catch-it-by-yourself-beings." In the process of this cunning transition, we have lost the art of creating and maintaining relationships.

We are a society in a hurry. In a hurry *to where*, is anyone's guess, but our culture has been feeding and reinforcing the notion quite well. Businesses have preyed on the transformation of the family. Fast food chains soak up billions of our dollars annually, feeding our families on the run. In my parenting lifetime alone, I've watched the frozen dinner aisle at the grocery store grow from one compartment to multiple freezer lanes offering faster and faster ways to eat at home. Convenience stores have installed "pay at the pump" gasoline, so we don't have to spend one minute interacting with the cashier to pay the bill. "Call me on my mobile," because I don't have time to sit around and wait for your call. "Fax it to me" or "Zap it to me by e-mail," I can't wait until tomorrow to get it by snail mail. Moreover, if we want to feel good real fast, all we have to do is "snort a line" or "pop a pill" or better yet, shoot some instant happiness into our brains—I mean our veins. We are a society hooked on speed, and not only the narcotic variety. Simply put, we have become addicted to instant gratification. Waiting two minutes for the microwave to zap a cup of coffee for a "quick start" in the morning is too long. "My heavens, can't this thing read my mind? It should be hot the second I think it!"

The sad thing is, we're not yet happy, because fast is not fast enough. How fast do we have to run to feel fully satisfied?

In our quest to simplify our lives, we have actually made our lives more complex. We have created new problems for ourselves, not the least of which is how to unify a family while soaring through cyber-space.

As we transformed from a "whenever you can get around to it" horse and buggy society to an "I want what I want, when I want it, and I want it now" cyber-space society, we forgot to inform the attention-seeking, appreciation-needing, self-worth-craving human within us, that we would have to forego those basic needs in the transition.

Our needs and desires remain very old fashioned in the supersonic world we have created. Those basic needs belong to a long ago era, when John-Boy was a reality, not a nerd. While our bodies live in a society that ignores those needs, our minds and hearts belong to a warmer, caring age of long ago. Thus we are a frustrated lot.

How did this happen?

Obviously, we were in an Alice in Wonderland sleep-state. When we woke up the world had catapulted so far in a new direction, we could not catch up. It's downright frustrating not to be able to catch up. The very first victim was the family. Women needed "equality" with men. Men needed to be more "domesticated" like women. Children needed to be "self-esteemed" despite their actions. Various gurus told us we all needed to be "stress free" and "fulfilled!" We were supposed to be a "feel-good society," but instead felt frustrated.

What has clearly been the result of our frustration?

Divorce has quadrupled, youth violence has quintupled and suicide has increased ten-fold—especially among our youth. Parents don't know what to do with their children. Children sometimes figure out what to do with their parents—ignore them or kill them. Murder of parents by rage-filled children is more common than we would like to know. Road rage? Road rage wasn't even in our vocabulary ten years ago. What is road rage? It's wanting what I want when I want it and I want this road NOW, if I have to kill you to get it.

Our society has become a war zone. Murder at McDonalds. Gangs and gang wanna-be's, intimidating shoppers at the mall. Armed guards, surveillance cameras and metal detectors in most public places. Mass murder in schools—in nursery schools—even churches! We know all too well that every time we turn around, we are faced with a new kind of terrorism, and all too much of it comes from internal—not foreign—sources! There are no safe havens left for our children. Even before the days of international terrorism, guns were resolving the problems. We apparently have lost the ability to communicate with words.

In all that running and racing to keep up, we lost sight of what we were really chasing. Do we even know what it was? Is this where we wanted to be?

First Forgive

*As far as the east is from the west, so far hath he removed
our transgressions from us.*   —Psalm 103:12

Before venturing any further down the parenting road, do yourself a favor and lighten your already staggering load. First, forgive all parenting mistakes. Forgive the mistakes your parents
made with you. Forgive the mistakes your parenting-partner makes
when you've "told them so." Forgive the mistakes your children make
when "they know better," and above all, forgive yourself for the mistakes you make.

Bearing grudges, harboring malice, seeking revenge and wal-
lowing in self-loathing are only heavy burdens weighing you down
with distractions, and draining your energy for the real job at hand.
Three women have reminded me of the truth in this. I believe their
messages are useful. All are mothers of children viciously murdered
in senseless, brutal crimes. As a mother, I can think of no pain greater
than losing a child, especially losing a child in such an evil, senseless
manner. My heart breaks for all of them.

The first is mother to the victim of a youth I worked with at a
maximum-security unit for juvenile offenders. She irately announced
on television in several interviews, even nationally, that her sole mission in life is to assure that the perpetrator of her daughter's murder
remains in prison as long as the law allows. She vehemently expressed
a desire for the perpetrator to suffer as much as she has suffered. She
reported having involved herself in victims' rights groups, not for the
mutual support they provide, but solely for the purpose of assuring

that all perpetrators of crimes are punished to the maximum extent of the law. She stated that she intends for this endeavor to become her "life's mission."

The second woman, I fleetingly met at a community meeting. She was outgoing and bubbly, and reached out to help another woman having difficulties whom she had met only that morning. When she handed me her card, I noted she was running for a local political office. The woman she had reached out to help was not even a citizen of this country. Obviously, her efforts were heartfelt and not a ploy to gain a vote. Later that week while channel surfing, I saw her again on television. She was on a panel of candidates for the office she was seeking. Briefly, I heard this remark: "When my daughter was murdered..." I listened, she said little more about the murder, instead emphasizing the need to intervene in our children's lives and to work to establish meaningful programs and laws to minimize such tragedies in the future.

The third woman I do not know, but saw her powerful story on a TV newsmagazine. An intruder robbing houses for drug money randomly selected her daughter's house, entered while she was at home, and savagely murdered her daughter. From the outset, this woman sought revenge. When the perpetrator received the death penalty, she was pleased and made plans to have the satisfaction of watching him die at his execution. As the time for his execution drew near, she realized she was not yet satisfied. She insisted on meeting the perpetrator, face to face. When that meeting was finally negotiated, she traveled to the prison, intent on berating the man. Instead, their full-day visit ended with his deeply felt apology, her expression of forgiveness and their praying together.

While it is devastating to even consider the idea, if you were forced to walk in the shoes of any of these women, whose shoes would you prefer to be walking in? Despite the unspeakable tragedy each experienced, which of these women do you think might be experiencing the greatest peace? Which might you expect to be leading a productive, satisfying life, despite her tragedy? Which might have the most emotional freedom and energy to adequately care for any remaining children?

Hopefully, nothing you or anyone in your life has done, or ever will do, is as devastating as the transgressions experienced by these women. Regardless, if there are those who can forgive such tremendous wrongdoings, what will it take for you to forgive yourself and those around you for the missteps of everyday life?

When you forgive, you empty yourself of the debilitating heaviness produced by thoughts and feelings of anger and vengeance and you clear out space to fill up with much more useful equipment. The hope here is that you will use that freed up space to fill up on some 20/20 hindsight, to help you avoid some potentially damaging, and certainly painful, bumps along the parenting highway. Free of the distractions and energy drain of unforgiveness you are already better prepared to set your sights.

Defy Disposable Values

For they have sown the wind, and they shall reap the whirl-
wind ...   *— Hosea 8:7*

Posted on my office wall is a saying I read somewhere. It reads, "If you aim at nothing, you will hit it." Before we can get where we want to be, we must determine where it is that we are going. A road map helps. The problem is, parenthood comes without road maps, guidebooks or instruction manuals and certainly without guarantees. We are simply supposed to "know how," by virtue of being handed a warm bundle. Where do we find the instructions?

Experience is the best teacher. Most unfortunate is the fact that you are going to make many painful mistakes on the parenting journey in order to ever get that experience. Hindsight is, after all, 20/20. Regardless of preparation and continuing education, there will be mistakes. The real goal is to minimize the mistakes.

Take aim. Know where you are going, from wherever you are starting this journey.

How do you set your sights to take aim, when you have become accustomed to racing, with total abandon, through life?

It is important to acquire a firm focus on those things that are most important to you. Then when you set your sites, you have an actual target at which to aim.

Recall that in our lifetime there have been societies dictating how their citizens must live. What if we found ourselves living under the rule of a society that dictates our values? "What if?" is really not the question any more. We do not have to look all the way to the other side of the world to find oppressive dictators. We have clearly been living in a society that dictates our values through something we have come to call "The Powers That Be."

You don't believe it? Let's just take a moment to visit "The Powers That Be." To do that with the proper perspective with which we generally view "The Powers That Be," you must first put on a set of blinders. You know—the kind we occasionally see on a horse pulling a carriage, so that he is not distracted by all that goes on around him.

Are your blinders carefully in place?

Okay! Now looking straight ahead and avoiding any distraction, picture in your mind just what these "Powers That Be" are.

"The Powers That Be" are deceptively undetectable creepy crawly critters, silently oozing slimy penetrating whispers of sweet enticing pleasantries and heartwarming comforting promises, which they have no intention of keeping. Get a clear picture of them in your mind's eye.

But wait! "The Powers That Be" are now emerging from the shadows as powerful gargantuan invisible giants, capable of snuffing out hopes and dreams by eradicating values and morals one baby-step at a time. Do you see them straight ahead, trampling your own hopes and dreams?

We occasionally get an evasive glimpse of them if we look very carefully. "The Powers That Be" are "those people," "the big guns," "the good old boys (and gals)" to whom we—you and I—and generations before us, have consistently relinquished our own seats of powerful honor for guarding and guiding our lives as well as the lives of our children. With your blinders on, can you see them sitting way up there at the glittery top with their toothy Cheshire grins?

Amazing! With all that power, few seem to know who these "Powers That Be" are, with their tremendous influence to overtake minds and practices—especially the minds and practices of impressionable children. Stealthily, "The Powers That Be" come and whisper their dictates for our fashion—even right down to the popular color of the day; for our reading material—now primarily at a sixth grade level; for our viewing pleasure—increasingly violent and sexually tantalizing. With your blinders on and looking straight ahead, just imagine what "The Powers That Be" may be taking away from us at this minute, as they scurry around to the right and left of you, dictating not only your purchasing preferences, but ultimately your manner of thinking.

Keep your blinders on tightly as you become increasingly aware that without constant, careful guarding "The Powers That Be" are all around you, trampling your territory with their slipshod baby-steps, telling and selling their wares, and like ever-absorbing sponges, our society is buying in and beginning to live as though the messages of "The Powers That Be" are gospel. Just imagine the alterations of the gospel "The Powers That Be" make with each tiny baby-step!

Before taking off those blinders and viewing exactly where it is that "The Powers That Be" have led you, keep in mind that as the years have passed, "The Powers That Be Gospel," for a vast portion of our society, has come to read something like, "The younger a kid is, the more adorable they will be while wearing revealing adult clothing designed to expose the most of their body parts." For many it continues to read, "Leave those poor kids alone, they need to be kids and reading and writing aren't kid-stuff—History! Erase ten or twelve chapters. That's too much to learn, and then write it in baby talk so the poor kids don't have to stretch their minds too far." "Aren't those the funniest adult role models you've ever seen? I laugh my head off watching them booze it up every Friday night. What a hoot it is watching them curse and cavort in front of their kids! I laughed myself silly!"

Off with the blinders and eyes wide open now! Look all around at the silent hideous messages left by "The Powers That Be," slithering in and never out, incessantly heaping increasingly insurmountable mountains of drivel that society keeps buying. Where are the guards?

When was it that we let our guard go and relinquished good values and morals to "The Powers That Be" who so insidiously extracted them from our lives without our even batting an eye? All it takes is the blink of an eye, and those gargantuan invisible "Powers That Be" move right in and take one more baby-step, as they trample on your tediously and lovingly cultivated values.

Keep alert! With your eyes wide opened you can interrupt the vicious devastation of "The Powers That Be."

After imagining handing over your most precious values to an invisible hulking "Powers That Be" Giant, you are probably left with a sinking, empty feeling. Even though this was only an imaginary exercise, considering what it represents makes it all too serious. Even though you may have been carefully guarding your territory with every ounce of strength within you, remember that your children have been exposed to a larger society, and we live in a society that has been relinquishing values for decades—in fact, much longer. Just imagine. At the speed our society is racing, we have not been watching as "The Powers That Be" have stripped us of treasures we once so dearly valued. We never noticed it was happening.

Socrates is attributed with having said, "What is happening to our children?" I was in high school when someone passed that statement around as a joke. We all laughed and I am sure many generations have laughed at that statement. I don't think we're laughing any more.

As our society has covertly and insidiously disposed of values bit-by-bit, decade after decade, we have been left with enormous segments of our society feeling emotionally empty. When we are emotionally empty, we can barely sustain ourselves, let alone others. Therefore, we have little to nothing left to give toward building and maintaining relationships, even relationships with our own children. Instead, our focus turns solely to trying to fill up that uncomfortable gnawing emptiness. That is when we begin stuffing without looking, or even caring what it is we stuff inside ourselves.

Just as a starving man stuffs in food to overcome hunger, emotionally starved people stuff in everything that looks good, sounds good or feels good, to fill the emotional void. There is no time to think or care about the quality of food being devoured. There is no time to check whether the food is spoiled or contaminated. There is no time to even consider the results of stuffing on a starving stomach. The results are distressing: sick, bloated, distended stomachs, still unsatisfied and aching for relief.

What do we do to relieve the resulting discomfort?

Stuff in more of the same! We want to taste something. We want to feel full. We want the bloating to go away.

Where is this emotional void from disposed values leading us?

The headlines tell us exactly where it is leading us—Bombings in our schools! Random murders in our streets. Domestic violence by youth on parents is increasing at alarming rates. Teenage suicide epidemics—indeed, teen suicide pacts! Parents burying children at tender ages!

Where will this all end?

Obviously, it will end in self-destruction. That is, unless we grit our teeth, roll up our sleeves, apply the elbow grease and work up enough sweat to get us off this road of disposable values.

Finding Courage

*...for verily I say unto you, if ye have faith as a grain of
mustard seed, ye shall say unto this mountain, remove
hence to yonder place; and it shall remove; and nothing
shall be impossible unto you.* — Matthew 17:20

Many can point out your flaws, make suggestions, offer some tools, but you must be the one to make the difference. The road will get very rough at times. It will require patience beyond measure. This is going to take a dedication like you may never have known. It will take a commitment you may never have exercised. It is going to take a great deal of courage on your part, to work your way to smoother ground.

From where will you drum up the courage you will need to hang on through rocky, rough terrain?

Faith and prayer!

I do not say this lightly, or flippantly. I say this, because I know clearly, from 20/20 hindsight, that faith and prayer work. In fact, regardless of your intellect, experiences, diplomas or any other worldly resources, while I cannot explain the supernatural reason for it, I know without a doubt, that when the parenting road gets rough, faith and prayer are the only things that will help.

This is not easy. Having faith is next to impossible when you feel yourself falling off cliffs and sliding down embankments, while you are struggling to navigate rocky roads with children in tow. Turning to prayer in those difficult times may be the last thing on your mind. I can only assure you that if you will take the first step, prayer will smooth the way.

Years ago at a prison ministry volunteer appreciation banquet, a young man who had served time in prison shared his testimony. His clean cut, boyish looks belied the story he was telling. He described years of living in filth and squalor, while stealing and robbing for drug money. He described vacated, rat-infested buildings as his home. He talked of cardboard boxes as his bed. He described filthy, matted hair, decaying teeth, oozing sores and collapsed veins. He reported his involvement in a vicious crime that landed him in prison for many years.

His testimony, to the group, related to a miracle from God that freed him from an impossible prison term. His testimony, for me, was quite different.

At the end of his testimony, this young man added one final comment that I've carried deep within my heart for the many years that I traveled rocky roads with my children. He said, "I praise God for a mother who prayed for me for fifteen years."

Fifteen years! How could I survive fifteen years with my son?

Life had been filled with many challenges: divorce; single-parenting; raging warfare with the "ex;" battles over custody of the children; cancer; poverty; food stamps; working multiple jobs just to pay the bills; broken-down cars and four children reacting to the chaos and confusion.

Maybe, if I'd prayed earlier I would have avoided some of those catastrophes. "Better late than never," I told myself. I did not know how to pray, but I began.

Months later I told an elderly woman at a Bible study group that prayers did not seem to be helping my son. He was still so troubled. This woman with a seasoned prayer life told me, "You just keep on praying and going to church and one day your son will ask to go with you." I continued praying, but in truth, while I did not say it out loud, I was thinking, "I doubt it."

I remember the first Sunday I was dressed and leaving for church. My son was lying on the couch watching television. He mumbled, "Where ya' goin'?" Having learned to decipher the slurred words of a defiant youth, I responded with hope, "To church, would you like to go with me?"

I won't even write the expletives that seethed from his mouth. To equate it with scenes from "The Exorcist" is sufficient. I did not respond, but left for church, saddened.

We repeated that scene and scenes like it, weekly. Months went by and I began to notice that the expletives were diminishing. Over a year passed. My prayers continued, but sometimes without much hope behind them.

Several more months passed when one night my son asked, "Are you going to church Sunday?" I curbed my impulse to express surprise at his question. "Yes, would you like to go with me?" "Yes." was his answer. He asked if his girlfriend could go with us, and of course I said, "Yes." I hid my joy from my son, but not from God. I praised Him gratefully.

On Sunday morning, my son's girlfriend called. She could not go with us to church because she had sprained her back trying to lift a stuck garage door. I just knew this would mean my son would back out of the trip to church. Holding my breath I asked him, "Are you still going?" Imagine my joy when he said, "Yes, of course."

Almost twenty years have passed since that first trip together to church with my oldest son. Since that time I've been blessed to see him baptized. I enjoyed the blessing of his church wedding to that same girlfriend. I've rejoiced at the church dedication of their first child. I've marveled at his dedication to achieving his college education and building a successful career. This past Christmas I had the joy of watching that very same son with his growing family, posing in a manger scene at their church. Brent was Joseph, his wife was Mary and their new baby boy was the Baby Jesus. That he dressed as The Easter Bunny for the church Easter egg hunt may be somewhat controversial, but nevertheless a blessing to me, when I recall how far that Easter bunny had come to hide those eggs. While he may or may not recognize prayer as the source of his transformation, I know my prayers were answered.

It has not all been easy. When one has traveled a rough road for many years, there are bound to be more bumps on the way to smoother terrain. There have been, and still are bumps—some of them huge. There have continually been prayers, and the road seems to be smoother for longer stretches between the bumps!

Would I have reached a smoother road without faith and prayer? I don't see how. Relationships, like houses, need foundations. I now know that I had no foundation upon which to build a relationship before I added the power of faith and prayer.

I recall Dale Evans Rogers once telling that she met a botanist at a party. In their conversation she made the comment, "People are so much like plants—they grow in the sunlight."

The botanist said, "No, that is not true. It is true people and plants are alike, but each grows in the darkness. In the light they take in the nutrients they need to grow, but it's only in the darkness that they can grow."

When I am in dark discomfort and distress, I would like to say I immediately turn to God. I know and admire others who do. However, it often takes me a time of questioning and fretting and even fuming to realize that the darkness is a new opportunity to grow. Once I finally recognize it, I can then use the darkness as a time to grow closer to the One who will undoubtedly make the light shine brightest.

Dark roads can create bright opportunities to build strong relationships. In my work in adoption there was an interesting rule of thumb. It may sound somewhat offensive, however, when a family adopted a child (especially an older child) and soon thereafter the child became ill—perhaps with chicken pox or the flu—we were actually pleased. This time of "darkness" provided a unique opportunity to accelerate bonding in the relationship. The "darkness" was an opportunity for the family to actively minister to their new child in a way that exhibited their care and concern most authentically and tangibly. At the same time, the "darkness" virtually forced the opportunity for the child to lean on his new family and experience for himself that they would care for him and protect him, even in dark times. The relationship would grow best in "darkness."

Before there can be a relationship, there must be a foundation upon which to build it. Faith and prayer confirmed by action, offer the strongest of foundations upon which a relationship can flourish. It may take a great deal of time in the darkness to build that foundation, but I would venture to say that the darkest roads can establish the strongest foundations. On long, dark roads carry this reminder: God's timing in answering prayers is perfect. He is never too early and He is never too late. (Isaiah 49:8; 60:22)

While we may feel ready, prepared, eager and anxious for a certain step in our journey, God has the full picture. It may be difficult to understand the roadblocks and detours thrown in our path. Often it is frustrating, even enraging to accept delays, especially delays in answers to prayers we believe are well intended and in the best interest of those for whom we have prayed. Only when we have crossed the hurdles and look back down the roads we have traveled, can we see where God has led us and even *why* He has led us through rocky terrain. Only then, can we understand the purpose for the obstacles.

God's answers to prayers are always right on time. Sometimes we are standing in His way and slowing Him down!

The Mirror's Reflection

Create in me a clean heart, O God; and renew a right spirit within me. — *Psalm 51:10*

How often when seeking answers to prayers have I cried out to God, "Speak louder, I can't hear you!" Then, when the dust settles, I see it isn't God who is not talking loud enough. It's me, looking in the wrong direction.

For years we looked at Brent as the problem. If we could just "fix" Brent, our problems would vanish. I now know that was not true; the problem was much more pervasive. Families are systems; each part depends on, and reacts to, the others. If one part suddenly changes, all of the other parts are actually forced to adjust, to fit and work comfortably with the new dynamics of the changed part in the system.

I was once advised by the mechanic to change one of the belts in my car. He said it was cracked and would soon break. "It's always something!" I thought, as I went back to my office, where I consulted with our automobile guru, Frank. Surely, Frank would know a way to resolve this problem without it costing me an arm and a leg.

Frank informed me that indeed, I definitely needed to change that belt. Then, he added something I certainly did not want to hear. Frank said it would behoove me to change all of the belts in the car. He explained in detail that changing one belt alone would put so much strain on the others; they would all stop doing their jobs, as well.

Family systems are similar to the system in our car. If one part changes, it increases the potential that, sooner or later, other parts will be pressured to change their previous method of functioning. Sometimes the change can be for the better.

It seemed to me that when our family's "mother part" began changing, the "Brent part" stopped squeaking as loudly.

I know people used to think his name was "NOBrent!" When I finally recognized that fact, I began looking for opportunities to call him "YESBrent." It was not easy, because:

1)   I was in the habit of calling him, "NOBrent." Habits are hard to break.

2)   Brent expected me to call him, "NOBrent." It had become his comfort zone.

3)   I had never actively looked for opportunities to call him, "YESBrent." I had to learn how, and learning would take time.

Although there were only the two of us in the room, I felt absolutely ridiculous the day I heard myself saying with total sincerity, "Thank you Brent for turning on the light." I felt even more ridiculous saying, "Thank you Brent for shutting the door." These were things any ordinary human being would do under the particular circumstances. However, with those simple "thank you's" to build on, I began changing the way I interacted with Brent, and Brent apparently began changing the way he expected me to respond.

As I prayed and became more responsive to God's direction and desire for my life, I changed. I changed the way I thought, the way I acted, and the way I reacted to Brent. As long as I refused to waver in my change, Brent was essentially "pressured" to find a new way to respond to the new me!

When all was said and done, I believe Brent began to sense something in me had changed. At some point he seemed to realize that old behaviors were not so effective any more and he might get as much, if not more, nourishment from a "yes" than a "no." Eventually, he seemed to start trying the "yeses" on for size. Little by little, "Yes" seemed to fit at least as well, if not better than "No."

Why can't the child change first?

Parents are the mirrors. Children are the reflections of those mirrors. Children do not know how to act and react, until parents reflect it to them. If children are the reflections of their parents' mirrors, is it then not puzzling when those parents become angry at how their children reflect them?

I can honestly say that as a mirror, I needed serious re-silvering.

One evening while I was bathing Kayla, then almost three, she asked for something that was in another room. Being a cautious mother, I did not want to leave her alone in the tub, so I called to my husband to bring the item.

Suddenly, a bellowing came from the tub. I turned to watch my not yet three-year old bellowing with a sharp, angry tone, "JOE! JOE! JOE!"

My first reaction was to reprimand her. "Don't call Daddy by his first name. You call him 'Daddy'." But, the minute I started to say, "... and we don't yell like that," I realized she was imitating me.

Did I really sound like that? You bet I did. How else would a not yet three year old, know how to turn "Joe" into a three-syllable word? It made me think more than twice about how I looked and sounded to my children.

I struggled to become a saintly woman. Regardless of my anger, I responded in quiet, docile tones. I determined I would never again yell from one room to another. Unfortunately, that was the wrong response. Instead of exploring the basis for the angry, sharp yelling, I was dealing only with my behavior on the outside. It was years before I would even be ready to acknowledge the anger raging inside.

What if your own mirror is in good shape, but your children seem to be reflecting someone else's tarnished and peeling mirror?

They probably are.

As children mature, the push and pull to gain independence leads them on a path through numerous other mirrors. At first they look to adult mirrors for their reflections—parents, teachers, baby-sitters, parents of friends, adult relatives. Then they begin noting that their peers are interesting mirrors to reflect. When they see something in the mirror that they like, they try it on. If they like how it looks, and especially if they gain approval for how it looks, they begin wearing it. You may never know they saw it, let alone bought it!

When children begin trying on other mirrors' reflections, parents must become more observant and more involved than ever. If they are not watching, their child may try on another mirror's tarnished, peeling silver and think it looks pretty good. Parents have to be there, armed and ready to brush on a fresh coat of silver. Be aware, one coat will never do the job. As long as you are a parent, you need to keep that re-silvering brush handy.

Many parents think they are relieved of most of the responsibilities of their job when they get their children off to elementary school. We taught them right from wrong—"don't touch," "don't break," "don't hurt." We taught them manners—"say please," "say thank you." Now they are ready to hit the road.

Wrong! Parenting is never—let me repeat: Parenting is never finished!

I don't know about you, but from time to time I still need parenting, and I certainly know my children still need parenting; and we are all well beyond six-years of age! If you have children, you are in the parenting business—for the duration.

The Parenting Business

For God is not the author of confusion, but of peace...
— I Corinthians 14:33

While I was building a career for myself, I made many parenting errors. Controversial as the subject is, I do believe there are working mothers (and fathers, too, of course) who are excellent parents. However, not everyone is suited for both activities, especially simultaneously. I would have done well to select one job or the other! Thus, I learned a lot about parenting from what I did wrong. So it is now with more than thirty-three years of 20/20 hindsight, that I am most grateful to say that despite my blips, bleeps and absolute mess-ups, I eventually learned that:

1) It is never too late to turn errors around.
2) Rocky starts can have happy endings.
3) Acquiring a new perspective is required to turn errors around, if we want to have those happy endings.

At my first social work job, the agency director announced that he had met a woman who considered parenting to be the family business. He felt her ideas on parenting were quite unique and invited her to provide a staff training session. This was more than thirty years ago, yet over the years I have thought of this training experience with increasing frequency.

Sally arrived with index cards outlining her presentation. "Quite organized for a housewife," I thought. She informed us that she and her husband considered parenting to be their primary job, and therefore they approached parenting as they would a business. As I recall, *at the time of this training their children, two boys and a girl, ranged in age from about three to seven.*

As the "director" and "assistant director" of their family business, Sally and her husband together developed their "mission statement" and wrote out their "business plan" and "job descriptions" for themselves and their family "staff." They held regularly scheduled "administrative meetings" at which they assessed the progress of their business. At these meetings they established "long term goals" for their family. Next, they established "short term goals" to maximize the potential for success of the long-term goals. They targeted "production areas" that they believed must be addressed to achieve these goals. As I remember, Sally outlined such areas as religion; education; social relations; talents and skills; recreation; finances, or using business terms as Sally did, "economic principles." Then she explained how each of these areas would be addressed at weekly family "staff meetings."

As "staff," their three children were responsible for "completing work assignments" necessary to help the "administrators" achieve the family business goals. Sally and her husband held "joint and individual staff development sessions" with their children to build their "job related skills" for achieving established goals. Dinnertime was diligently used for "staff discussions" focusing on issues related to the "family business."

There were numerous facets to Sally's "Parenting Business," and she spent four hours explaining her business to us. By the time she finished, I wondered whether purchasing a briefcase and calculator would in any way serve to make me a better parent!

At that time, Sally's ideas seemed at best unusual and intriguing. At worst, they seemed cold and calculated. In either case, her ideas seemed impractical. It seemed unlikely any other parent would buy in to her parenting business plan.

Now, with over thirty years of 20/20 hindsight of my own, I have to wonder whether Sally and her husband had some gift of foresight that the rest of us were lacking. While Sally's "Parenting Business" might seem somewhat stilted, it is evident that she and her husband were most serious about fully assuming their responsibilities as parents. Their plan certainly provides a new perspective for assuming the responsibility of "parent."

Each of us brings children into our family for very personal reasons. The problem is that most of us fail to realize the magnitude of responsibility that comes with the job of parenting. We rarely have the opportunity to practice parenting before hand. We may baby-sit or look after younger siblings; some might even have the benefit of a novel class offered in some schools. In such classes, a "pretend baby" is issued and the student must care for that "pretend baby" at all times, for a given number of days. The "pretend baby" is electronically calibrated to cry at various intervals, requiring immediate attention!

I was recently at a restaurant with friends, when one of them walked away suddenly. When he returned, we all asked what had happened. He said, "I just had to see if I saw what I thought I saw."

"What?" we asked in unison.

"I thought I saw this kid sitting at the bar with a baby."

"Well?" we queried.

"Aw! It was just one of those pretend babies they get at school. She said she had to report in class that she spent every minute with the pretend baby, so she brought it to the bar with her."

We all had to wonder if she would report on the location she had chosen to take her "baby."

While this "pretend parenting" program does have some good merits, if it is with that kind of parenting practice we enter parenthood, it is no surprise that we are stunned by the sharp reality of "real parenting." It is an old but true adage: "Children take far more than they give." Are any of us ever truly prepared for how much they take?

In more than thirty-three years of parenting, over twenty-five years of which include professional counseling, I have never met another "Sally." Therefore, I can only assume that the "Sally's" of this world are rarities. Most of us plunge headlong into parenting, only to realize we are unprepared. It is then that we must take a big step backward to adequately organize ourselves for the responsibility we undertook some time ago. We might organize formally, as did Sally and her husband, making charts and time-lines, setting goals and establishing individual responsibilities for overseeing the success of our Parenting Business or, we might organize less formally to assess and determine our direction. However, to effectively parent, organize we must!

It is highly recommended that your Parenting Business be managed on a regularly scheduled basis, with goals and plans **written** and frequently reviewed. To help you start putting your Parenting Business in writing, a pullout Parenting Business Start-Up Kit is provided for you at the end of the book. It's never too soon to start organizing, so pull it out and call for a family meeting. It is far too easy to become distracted and disorganized on the parenting highway. A tangible means of focus is virtually imperative to assure that everyone in the family is speaking the same language and heading down the same road.

Human Mirrors

For a just man falleth seven times and riseth up again...
— Proverbs 24:16

No matter how organized you become, every parent makes mistakes and some of them are REAL mistakes! It makes life a whole lot easier if you just accept it as fact: You will make mistakes. When you do, don't panic! Do what any reasonable adult would do—correct your mistakes by openly admitting them and apologizing for them.

Admit my mistake? Apologize to a child? Won't that diminish my authority?

No. In fact, it will increase your credibility and reinforce your authority.

You are the primary role model for your children. You are the "mirror" which they reflect; what YOU do, THEY will do! How you act and react is how your children will learn to act and react. It is therefore vital to establish the qualities you wish to instill in your children and model those qualities for them. Granted, it is much easier to do it right the first time, than to have to undo distasteful behaviors and re-establish the desired behaviors you want instilled in your children. However, although difficult, it is definitely possible to change directions if necessary.

Regardless of our own insecurities, as adults, we appear all-powerful to children. By virtue of our size alone, our words carry a great deal of weight, especially for very young children. Therefore, we must bear full responsibility for how our words and actions impact a child's life. If we realize we have said or done something that a child might interpret as hurtful, or that may possibly be harmful to our relationship with him in any way, it is our responsibility as the adult in the relationship, to remedy that action. We must help the child talk about it. The best door opener for such a conversation is an apology.

Perhaps the most important reason to apologize to a child for something we have done wrong, is to let him know that it is only human to make mistakes, and it is not only the right thing to do, but it is perfectly safe to take responsibility for the mistakes we make. In setting the example by apologizing, we let the child know that there is nothing wrong with admitting our mistakes, especially if we learn from them. It is so critical to help a child take responsibility for his behavior—but first we, the adults, must take responsibility for ours!

Of course, the most basic reason to apologize for something we've done wrong is that we expect our children to apologize for what they've done wrong. It is so basic, yet there are those who believe it diminishes an adult's authority to apologize.

One Sunday afternoon I was in the den when my daughter came in with her best friend. She announced they were going to the car wash to wash her car. For no rational reason, I said, "No, you aren't. You don't need to go to any car wash." I knew I was headed down the wrong road, but I was the parent, after all. I said it, now I needed to hold my ground. I couldn't indicate that I had made a huge mistake, and, I knew better!

Kayla was sixteen had her own car and I'd unnecessarily embarrassed her in front of a friend. She could easily take that car and leave. So, when she didn't argue, but turned on her heel and went back outside, I assumed she was gone. Now, I would have to deal with her disobedience.

Five minutes later she came back into the den. I was shocked! What was she still doing there?

"Why can't I take the car to the car wash?"

Prideful, I thought I had to stand by my decision. Backing down would lead to problems with my authority. Since I had no real reason, I gave her the all time parental cop-out: "Because I said so, that's why." Again, she turned on her heel and went back outside.

I knew then that she really was going to defy me. I'd given her no rational reasoning and I'd given her no alternatives. Essentially, I had backed her into a losing corner. All she had to do was turn the key in the ignition and we'd both be in losing corners. Why, oh why had I ever said "no" in the first place? Then, why did I make matters worse when I had a chance to turn them around? All I had to do was say, "I'm sorry, of course you can go wash your car. I don't even know why I said 'no' in the first place."

Another five minutes went by and Kayla was back inside standing at the kitchen sink. She took a sponge and cleaner from under the sink and without a word went back outside and washed her car in the driveway. I was shocked! What in heaven's name would have caused her to accept my irrational response?

Later, I felt a need to apologize for my unnecessary, if not irrational actions. I asked Kayla why she hadn't gone to the car wash, despite me. She told me that I rarely said 'no' and that I was usually fair in my decisions with her. So, even though she had not understood, she thought I must have had a good reason for my decision or I would not have told her not to go.

Two things strike me most from that experience. The first is that somewhere along the line I took someone else's 20/20 hindsight and taught myself not to say "no" to my children, unless it was absolutely necessary. Impulsively and repeatedly saying "no" to a child diminishes a parent's credibility. It sets up a wall of distrust between the parent and child. The child learns to stop asking—stop asking anything, because the answer is going to be "no." We must be prudent in using the word "no" in our interactions with our children. The more we say "yes," the greater the impact when we must say "no."

The second thing that strikes me about the car washing experience is that if we are typically reasonable, fair and rational with our children, we don't become pushovers for them. On the contrary, we earn their respect. Then, when we momentarily lapse and are faced with humbly apologizing, they respect us enough to forgive us.

Super-Human Mirrors

Pride goeth before destruction, and a haughty spirit before
a fall.   — *Proverbs 16:18*

At the juvenile institutions where I've worked, the major conflicts I encountered were not with the youth, but with adult staff who insisted on "not backing down" despite having made clearly baseless decisions. I consistently found that when I treated the youth with respect, which meant occasionally apologizing to them for something I did wrong, they treated me with respect.

Many staff, and indeed the administrators of one facility, espoused the philosophy that "in front of children, adults never do anything wrong." Unfortunately, many parents hold this same conviction. Not only is that unrealistic and youth don't buy it, but it makes life for the adult very tough. Perfection is beyond my ability. Why would I want to put that kind of burden on myself, by placing myself in the impossible position of maintaining the pretense of being something I can never be? More importantly, why would I ever harm a child and not apologize for it?

As a clinician and administrator at maximum-security facilities for juvenile offenders, I had many opportunities to gather a virtual encyclopedia of harmful comments adults had made to children—comments eventually defining the lives of these young people. However, there is one particular comment that remains so etched in my mind, it now defines my interaction with all children.

I was observing a caseworker helping a group of about twenty boys work through a problem. At one point I interjected a comment to one youth, something like, "Eugene, you are so capable of positive leader-ship. Why aren't you helping your peer?"

Eugene scowled and spewed his words at me. "Get off it, Miss! I ain't never going to amount to nothin'! There's nothin' you can say to make me amount to anything, so just quit trying!"

Where Eugene's response came from was anyone's guess. It had nothing to do with the problem at hand. In fact, it was disrespectful. I was at a crossroad and needed to make a decision about which di-rection to go. I could address the behavior or address the comment. I chose to see this as an opportunity to open a dialogue. I ignored the behavior and pursued.

"Why do you say that, Eugene?" I asked.

I can hear him to this day and quote him precisely as his angry, stinging words echo in my ears.

"My first grade teacher told me I was never going to amount to nothin', so I'm not!"

Ten years earlier a teacher, of all people, made one comment that became the total definition of one child's life. For ten years he buried inside himself the pain created by that comment, until it totally de-fined for him who he was.

What does this have to do with apologizing to a child?

What if Eugene's first grade teacher had acknowledged she made a hurtful comment? What if she had taken only a moment to say, "Eu-gene, I am so sorry I said that? You have all the ability in the world to become anything you want to be. I wanted so much for you to see that for yourself, that I said the wrong thing. I'm really sorry."

If that apology had come, how do you think Eugene might have incorporated that comment into his life experience? Might the defi-nition of his life have been quite different? Might Eugene have told himself that teachers are human and make mistakes just like he did? Had his teacher apologized, Eugene might have had the opportunity to tell himself, "If she made a mistake and is a teacher, just think what I could become with all the mistakes I've made!" More importantly, had the apology been made, perhaps Eugene would have recognized the safety in acknowledging his own mistakes, giving him more con-fidence to take responsibility for his own behaviors.

We will never know, because that apology never came. Instead, a primary role model in a child's life made one throwaway comment that turned a child's life sour. She was, after all, in a position of authority and power. In his mind, she was the one with all the answers or she would not have been in such a position. Who, otherwise, was this six-year old child to believe? With an apology, the experience might have turned a child's life in an entirely different direction. With an apology, Eugene might have been preparing to head off to college, instead of sitting in a juvenile prison.

The "Eugene's" of this world are many. In fact, in our own ways each of us is a "Eugene." Not one of us has escaped painful life experiences. As we go through life we are inevitably firmly planted in the paths of others who insensitively throw barbs, frighten, abandon or reprimand us in ways that scar us. This inclination to harm one another has existed since the moment God said, "Don't eat" and the snake said, "Eat," then Eve said, "Eat" and Adam ate! (Genesis 3) It is unlikely the inclination to harm one another will disappear, at least in our lifetime. Therefore, we must learn ways to combat this inclination in our own lives and the lives of our children!

Here is what happens when a damaging comment is hurled out into space. It lands!

Although you cannot see it coming, like a meteor plummeting to earth, it creates a huge crater. Never again will that unspoiled ground be the same. Over time, trees and bushes may spring up to surround it, hiding it from view. However, no matter how well hidden the meteor site becomes, the truth is, the crater is still there. It may take a machete to slash through the curtain of overgrown foliage to reach the crater, but the fact is that no matter how much we do to repair the crater, the scar is never fully erased. There are no easy solutions for eliminating any scar. As The Parenting Business CEO you can only prepare yourself to jump in and begin the process of erasing scars from wherever you find yourself.

Less Than Human
Mirrors

Little children, keep yourselves from idols. Amen.
— I John 5:21

Where did we get the notion that adults must be super-human? How did we come to believe adults, especially parents, do not make mistakes?

Would you agree that television had a great deal to do with that?

All of those thirty minute situation comedies have taught us that parents must not only have all the answers to resolve all the world's problems in less than thirty minutes, but they must also sing joyfully while scrubbing toilets and taking out garbage. Seeing this hour after hour, week after week, year after year, has conditioned many of us to believe relationships just happen; children always respond favorably to well-intended parents, and every problem has a simple solution. When we see that we are failing to live up to those arbitrarily established standards, we begin to feel inept and inadequate as parents.

A new term crept into our vocabulary in recent years—"dumbing down." A number of years ago, a wise and alert person pointed out to me how the role models we were seeing on television were "dumbing down" the American public. Slapstick humor has been with us for eons. With time, those slapstick characters have become dumber and dumber, until they actually called themselves exactly what they had become. Even when they were dubbed exactly who they were, our society bought it! The movie reflecting the antics of two dumb guys drew in millions of dollars at the box office and video counters, and they continue their outrageous popularity in re-runs on television.

The "dumbing down" process did not start, nor stop with just one movie. Before our eyes, in our own living rooms, head of household role models increasingly became depicted as slovenly, amoral characters and the brunt of their own children's ridicule. Respect flew out the window, as values were "dumbed down."

While some of us were possibly considering the deteriorating values reflected in our entertainment sources, we might not have noticed that even the commercials paying for those senseless shows were becoming just as amoral. Recently, a grandmother proudly reported a cute phrase from a relatively benign commercial that her young granddaughter was now using in conversation. I couldn't help reminding her that if the child was repeating that particular phrase, she undoubtedly had heard (and remembered) other less benign phrases from other commercials.

That kind of indoctrination very stealthily persuades us to agree with what the media has to offer. We don't even realize it is happening, so how can we combat it?

If you don't recognize and acknowledge that there is a problem, there is nothing to fix! It is not until the problem becomes totally unmanageable that someone says, "Stop!" And like me, some of us open our eyes to find ourselves in a bog up to our shoulders. At that point we have a critical decision to make; we can choose to remain stuck in the muck, or we can choose to find a way to dig ourselves out. Only if and when we make the decision to change directions, can we start the grim process of fighting our way upstream to cleaner waters.

We "dumbed down" so far that there has been a modest public outcry, and thankfully, we are finally seeing a burst of moral shows gaining public attention—and public appreciation. However, if we don't remain alert, we will fail to notice that "Duh & Duh-er" are still with us, and they will consume our lives before we notice! We must arm ourselves for combat against the indoctrination factor!

In some homes televisions or computers are full time baby-sitters. In others, they are educational tools. In yet other homes they serve as a companion, filling an emotional void. In even others, these electronic devices are the primary source of entertainment. There are homes that run the television and computer twenty-four hours a day as security devices and night-lights! The diversity of uses alone, says that people in those homes have choices about how these electronic devices will be used.

It does not matter which electronic gizmo we are talking about when someone says, "That TV show caused that kid to murder," "That video game influenced that kid to kill," or "That website gave him those violent ideas," because what we are really hearing is that a parent knew the child was repeatedly watching the television, playing the game, or entering a website and did nothing to stop it; or that a parent was unaware that their child was incessantly involving himself in a destructive behavior and did nothing to increase their own awareness, so they could stop it. All it takes is diligent observation and an off and on switch to exercise that responsibility.

YAABUT vs. AHHBUT
Mirrors

Behold, I set before you this day a blessing and a curse; A blessing, if ye obey the commandments of the Lord your God, which I command you this day: And a curse, if ye not obey the commandments of the Lord your God, but turn aside out of the way which I command you this day, to go after other gods, which ye have not known.
— *Deuteronomy 11:26-28*

I will risk making this next statement because, unfortunately, I believe it to be true. After working with juvenile offenders long enough, it becomes evident that somewhere along the line an adult or adults, usually a parent or parents, did not do their job effectively. Criminals do not grow up in vacuums; they grow up in families.

Families consist of a wide variety of unique individuals who make a broad range of choices in fulfilling their particular role in their family. Possibly, the most alarming role chosen in a family is that of the "YAABUT Parent." YAABUT Parents often make poor, sometimes dangerous, choices for their family.

For example, when a parent member of a family says about a child in that family: "YAABUT, he whines when I turn off the TV!" they are making a choice. When a parent member of a family says: "YAABUT, I'm really busy! I don't have time to monitor everything he looks at!" they are making a choice. When a parent member of a family says, "YAABUT, he goes to his friend's and plays those video games!" they are making a choice. Worse yet, when a parent member of a family says, "YAABUT, I don't want him mad at me!" they are making a very poor choice.

Effective parents cannot be pals and parents to their children simultaneously. Families require leadership. Leadership implies that one leads and one follows. The leader is the guide who establishes boundaries, while the follower *depends* on the leader to teach him those boundaries. In the family unit, the roles are well defined. Parents are endowed with the responsibility of leading—children are responsible for following.

"YAABUT" parents don't lead—they actually relinquish their leadership responsibilities by turning critical decision making responsibilities over to their children. To serve effectively as the CEO of your Parenting Business and guide your children safely, especially in these times of instability and confusion, you must make the firm choice to stop making excuses. Stop with all the "YAABUT's" and learn to say "AHHBUT"!

When a CEO of any business turns major decision-making over to his staff, what is likely to happen? It is highly likely that salaries will skyrocket, vacation time will exceed work time, coffee breaks will become perpetual and profits will diminish, resulting in the ultimate demise of the business. The same is true of the Parenting Business.

Children crave boundaries. Boundaries are in fact, a child's security blanket outside of bed. Yes, of course children will push those boundaries as far as they will stretch. That's expected as a child strives to achieve independence. However, there is a time and place for independence.

As the Parenting Business CEO, it is your responsibility to determine at what age your child is expected to become independent, and then to lovingly, but consistently establish and enforce clear boundaries that support that time frame. The further the boundaries are permitted to stretch, the further and faster your child will stray. Unless the leader guards and enforces the established boundaries, the follower will push the boundaries beyond recognition. That's when parents hear themselves saying, "I surely didn't raise you to behave that way."

No, we did not intentionally raise our children to behave outside the boundaries of our expectations. But, when we do not carefully guard our boundaries, the territory will be invaded and taken over by the opposition. It is our job as parents, to guard our children's boundaries diligently.

Prisons are overrun with YAABUT people, most of whom had YAABUT parents. My response to all YAABUT parents would be, "YAABUT, if you made that choice, you are responsible for the consequences—no excuses."

Never will you be the only influence on your child's boundaries, but once you have accepted the position of CEO in the Parenting Business, it is your job to be your child's greatest influence.

Celeste was assigned as my secretary when I first went to work at the juvenile facility. To be honest (and I know she would admit this herself) she was not the most skilled secretary. However, she had skills that far surpassed typing and filing. She was, and I am sure still is, a woman of strong faith.

Since Celeste had worked at the facility far longer than I had, she was very instrumental in helping me find my way through the maze of rules and regulations thought necessary for operating a facility for juvenile offenders. The paper work was staggering. Internal procedures were cumbersome and often perplexing. However, by relying on her patient and sensible guidance, I somehow managed to navigate myself to a comfort zone in my new job.

I would often walk into the office and find Celeste staring straight ahead with the countenance of an angel. As I grew to know her better, I came to understand that those were times she was deep in prayer, most often over a troubled youth on the campus or another distressing notice from administration about changes in procedures.

We developed a warm and friendly relationship that went beyond that of supervisor and employee. I knew that she struggled with being a working mother. She was not happy with having virtual strangers raising her three children, and not necessarily instilling the values she and her husband wished to instill in them. That struggle only intensified when she became pregnant with her fourth child. I, on the other hand, was struggling with the fact that she would be taking a six-week maternity leave. I had no idea how I would endure six weeks without her support and her continual on-site prayer.

Not long before the birth of the baby, she came to me with an announcement that saddened me deeply. "I never thought I would be able to stop working," Celeste told me. "With the children, the bills just keep piling up and we've had to have my income to just survive. Now that we're having another child, I just knew that my salary would be critical."

Knowing her as I now did, I knew what was coming, as she continued, "We have prayed and prayed about this, and while we have no idea how we'll make it, we believe strongly that the Lord wants me to stay home with the kids."

Knowing what was coming did not stop the cannon ball from landing solidly in the pit of my stomach! Beyond coming to rely heavily on Celeste as support for my work, I had come to rely on her heavily for emotional and spiritual support. My first selfish thought was that I would not be able to survive without her. My second thought was, "How will they survive without her income?" I knew they were careful with their money, but I was also aware of her husband's salary, as he worked with us at the juvenile facility. To top it off, they commuted almost an hour each way to work. I could not imagine raising four children, as I had already done, and commuting to work on what their income would become without her salary. I don't think I said anything aloud that was totally offensive, however I did encourage her to give this more thought and please, please, please reconsider.

Celeste held fast to her belief and became a stay-at-home mom. While I kept in contact with her by phone following the birth of the baby, I was not able to travel to see the baby for several months. Although she always reported that things were going well and they were not struggling financially, on the drive over I prepared myself to find hollow-eyed children huddled in dark and dreary surroundings with Celeste attempting to keep up her happy pretense. I stopped for a soda and snack as I entered her town, not wanting to deplete their budget further by taking food from them during my visit.

Oh, me, woman of little faith! What I learned in that one visit! Not only were the lights on and water running, but also, theirs was indeed a happy household. Miracle upon miracle had befallen this wonderful family. The landlord actually lowered the rent, for no particular reason, except to show his appreciation for their taking such good care of the boyhood home he had turned into rental property. A woman at their church remembered that Celeste had remarked how much she liked one of her dresses, and although she still enjoyed wearing it, she was compelled to give it to Celeste. She then thought that while she was going through closets, she might as well give Celeste all of her children's outgrown clothes and even found a few other dresses she thought Celeste might enjoy. The stories went on and on, until the hour grew late and Celeste pulled from the oven a most ample dinner that she had prepared especially for my visit.

My memory of that, my last face to face visit with Celeste and her family many years ago, is of a joy-filled home, with smiles and warmth and love to share and share and share. I never worried about Celeste any more, and I learned to lean harder on God, instead of Celeste, for my spiritual support. Her faithful decision blessed each of us.

I do not share Celeste's story to promote stay-at-home mothers, but more importantly, to say that when you are facing a dilemma, as was Celeste, you must start somewhere. I believe that Celeste's example confirms the importance of listening to what your heart is telling you and then stepping out in faith to act upon it. Faith is, after all, "the evidence of things not seen." (Hebrews 11:1) Unless you take the first step, there will be no resolution to any problem you may be facing.

$\sim$

There is not a parent in the world who does not know when their child is hurting. The problem is that parents don't take time to develop the ability to help that child ease his pain. They don't cultivate sensitivity to their children because they are not willing to invest the time or energy necessary to do so. As parents, we all too often become so overwhelmed by our own problems or so caught up in our own activities, that we push away concerns about our children as we try to meet our own needs. Then, if we don't quickly see a simple solution to make a problem go away, we risk becoming YAABUT parents, leaving our children to find the means to sooth their own pain. The results can, and most often do, become heartbreaking.

While I only met Amber briefly one recent Christmas when I went to visit my daughter in Oregon, I know she is the daughter of YAABUT parents.

Her social worker told us that she had grown up somewhere in the Northeast. Apparently her parents had numerous financial, marital and personal problems that consumed their time and energy. Their problems went without resolution, and therefore only increased as Amber grew up.

As Amber grew into an attractive, active teenager, her parents had become so engrossed in dealing with their own problems that they

*barely noticed her comings and goings in the house. They hardly no-
ticed when the body piercing and tattooing began. They hardly noticed
when she began staying away all night. They hardly noticed her bleary
eyes and slurred speech when she was at home. YAABUT, her parents
were so involved in their own miseries, they hardly noticed when her
overnight absences turned into a full week, although when they finally
did notice, they reported her missing.*

*At fifteen, Amber found her way across the country. Portland, Or-
egon for some unknown reason had become a hub for runaway teens and
drug addicts. While adults may have been looking the other way and
saying, "YAA, these derelicts may look freaky, BUT they don't bother us,"
these teens were not only dying their hair green and purple and piercing
their tongues and cheeks, but shooting up regularly with heroin and
drowning themselves in other street drugs, as they slept in shop doorways
on the streets. "YAABUT, they didn't hurt anyone," thought the pass-
ers-by. So, at the time, Amber holed up in some doorway shelter with
friends she had met on the street and remained there for several months.*

*Finally, the police picked her up. Being underage, she was turned
over to social services. Social services placed her in a foster home, while
they attempted to locate her parents. When they were eventually located, her parents were too drained by their own problems to respond.
In fact, if I remember correctly, they told social services they did not
want Amber back home. So, she remained in the foster home. While
the foster parents attempted to provide Amber with shelter, safety and
some guidance, she felt drawn to return to her comfort zone with her
"street family." One dark night, she stole the foster family's car and
raced back to the places where she felt accepted. In the process she to-
taled the car.*

*As she lay in the hospital, her parents remained incapable of re-
sponding to her cries for help. Social services now became her legal
guardian and the Christmas I met Amber, my daughter and her husband had "adopted" her for the holiday, in an attempt to bring her a
bit of holiday cheer.*

*Laden with brightly wrapped packages, we walked into the nurs-
ing home with the social worker. She briefly prepared us for the visit,
saying, "If you can get past the outside, you'll find Amber's a wonderful young lady."*

She led us into a large room at the end of the long hallway. There

was an empty hospital bed in the far corner. Amber was up and pre-
pared for the visit. She was dressed all in purple, had shocking pink
and orange hair and countless silver studs protruding from her ears,
eyebrows, cheeks and tongue. YAABUT, there was more. As a result
of the car accident two years before, Amber was now quadriplegic,
confined to a wheelchair, unable to feel or move any part of her body
from her neck down. Short of a miracle, she would remain that way
for the rest of her life.

YAABUT responses to our children are unacceptable. To effectively
and safely raise our children, we must learn to use another, more productive, alternative. Like Celeste, we must learn to say "AHHBUT!"

For Celeste, "YAABUT I can't afford to stop working," became,
"AHH, the budget might be strained, BUT the Lord will help us find
a way." Can you imagine what a positive message Celeste and her
husband sent to their children, just by saying, "AHHBUT"?

Unfortunately, for the Ambers of this world, their parents can't or
won't jolt themselves loose from the YAABUT's. I was so grateful to
learn that despite her YAABUT parents, Amber herself had come to say,
"AHH, I'm confined to this wheelchair and totally dependent on others,
BUT I have a good mind and I'm going to use it to its greatest potential!" Her goal? To go to college to become a forensic psychologist!

It is not easy to transform from a "YAABUT" to an "AHHBUT"
Parent. It is not easy, but with faith, prayer and a good amount of
elbow grease, it can happen.

Not only can a Parenting Business CEO become AHHBUT about
their parenting responsibilities, they can also become AHHBUT about
the way they interact with their child. This is when parents turn the
tables on YAABUT children (children who may have wandered out
of control) and say, "AHH! I hear you, BUT that's not how we do it in
this family any more," and the dialogue can begin:

Child: "YAABUT all my friends are getting a new Zim
           Zam scooter!"

Parent: "AHH! That may be true, BUT running to the store
           on a whim is not how we are going to do it in our
           family any more."

Child: "YAABUT, they'll think I'm stupid if I don't get the
           new Zim Zam Scooter. They all have one! Do you
           want me to look stupid?"

Parent: "AHH, I certainly don't want you to look stupid, BUT I also need to be responsible with decisions about our money. So, we are going to change our way of doing things."

Child: "YAABUT, I want the Zim Zam Scooter in time for the competition next week."

Parent: "AHH, you want to enter a competition, BUT we aren't able to fit a new scooter into our budget right now."

Child: "YAABUT, you just don't care if I look like a fool on my old Slim Slam Scooter."

Parent: "AHHBUT I do care! I care a lot, so I'll tell you what; if you can help me find a way to stretch our budget so we can afford that special scooter, we might be able to work this out."

Child: "YAABUT, I'm too young to get a job. Besides, I couldn't earn that much money in two weeks, even if I started working today."

Parent: "AHH, you are too young to get a job, BUT perhaps you can think of some other way we could free up some of our budget for that scooter."

Child: "YAABUT, that means I'd probably have to give up something else.

Parent: "AHH! BUT that's a choice you will have to make if you really want that scooter."

Child: "YAABUT, it would probably be giving up going to the movies on Saturday, and I really like to go with my friends."

Parent: "AHH, you seem to be very concerned about what your friends are thinking about you, BUT it sounds like you are going to have to make a very difficult decision if we are going to resolve this problem."

Child: "YAA, I guess I could give up one movie a month maybe, BUT just until the scooter is paid for."

Parent: "AHH! That might work, BUT let's talk about it more so we can work out all the details."

Becoming an AHHBUT Parent takes sacrifice. It requires a major sacrifice of your time. It requires a major sacrifice of your patience. It requires a major sacrifice of your faith, believing that things can improve. AHH, that may be the greatest, BUT most rewarding, sacrifice of all. (Genesis 22)

Desensitizing Mirrors

And I will give them one heart, and I will put a new spirit
within you; and I will take the stony heart out of their flesh
and will give them a heart of flesh. — Ezekiel 11:19

Here is another exchange I had with Eugene several weeks after his disclosure about his first grade teacher. He was describing his home.

"We always lived in Fifth Ward. I mean my grandma, my momma and us kids. When we were little they used to let us run around there, but not anymore. It's real boring there. We gotta' stay inside all the time."

"Why is that?"

"Since I was six they wouldn't let us go outside anymore."

"Why, Eugene?"

"There was this time I was playing marbles with this kid and he just fell over. We was just shooting marbles in a circle on the ground, you know? He was just five years old and all of a sudden he was just lying there! I tried to get him up, but I couldn't. He wouldn't get up!" Eugene related, suddenly becoming emotional.

"What happened to him?"

Eugene's voice hardened. *"That was the first time I saw a dead body."*

That conversation took place following the Rodney King assault trial, the resulting riots and vicious beating of truck driver, Reginald Denny. When Eugene made that statement, "the first dead body," I recalled my own reaction to watching those beatings on television.

The first time I saw the videotape of the police beating Rodney King, I winced, virtually feeling every blow and kick. I was sickened and angry. The second time I saw it, I winced again in disbelief. The third and fourth times I saw the same video, I grimaced and shook my head, saying, "How awful." The tenth time I said something like, "That was really bad." The twentieth time I said, "I wish they'd quit showing that." By twenty-five, I began channel surfing: "Boring!"

So it was with the Reginald Denny beating. I was watching television when the live shots came of men dragging the driver from his truck, and then beating him with bricks. I heard the gasps of the helicopter reporter and gasped in horror myself. I felt every blow. I was horrified and appalled. Day and night the television stations ran the video of that horrendous beating, over and over and over again. By the third or fourth day, already primed by the Rodney King media coverage, I was channel surfing.

Does that mean I am an insensitive, hardened, uncaring individual?

No. It means that I too, have been desensitized—a variation of being "dumbed down."

I suppose it is similar to the desensitization that helps medical personnel deal with bloody, mangled, dying and dead bodies. To protect yourself from the emotional pain of what you are seeing, you must find a way to deaden the horrific feelings more and more to just survive, let alone assist. The more horror we see, the more we protect ourselves from it. The more upsetting the horror is to us, the more we turn off our feelings. The vicious cycle begins. The more we turn off our feelings, the easier it becomes to turn them off each time we are faced with another traumatic situation.

Add to that, television and violent video games. Over and over blood is splattered; fractured bodies fall; evil looking weapons roar. Over and over you are the perpetrator of that gore, albeit vicariously. Over and over it is no longer bodies falling and blood spurting. It's a game. The game is to see how many bodies you can topple and how much blood you can spill. Bodies and blood become numbers. Your focus is "numbers." Your goal is to get higher and higher "numbers." To do that, you must topple more and more bodies and shed more and more blood, and you are always trying to top your previous "numbers."

Can desensitized kids even discern real from fictional? It all starts to feel the same.

Guns? We could just collect all the guns and our world would definitely be a kinder, safer place.

In reality, killing is the real problem, not guns. Guns may make it easier, but when a desensitized person gets the notion to kill, they will kill.

William and two other boys were out riding around one night. They got bored and decided they needed some money to play video games or "do something."

One of the boys had done some yard work for an elderly couple and he knew where they kept some refundable beverage bottles. They decided to sneak on the property, steal the bottles and cash them in for some change for the video games.

They turned off the headlights and the engine and coasted into the driveway. They got out of the truck and headed for the stash of bottles. Suddenly one of the boys said, "Hey! There might be money inside."

The adrenaline started pumping. "Yeah! Let's do it!"

It was late and the house was dark. The boys thought the old couple would be sleeping. One of them broke a window and opened the back door. As they went inside, they saw the old couple with their backs to them, sitting side by side on the couch watching television in the dark. They were old and hard of hearing. The volume on the TV was turned up loud. The old couple had never heard their house being invaded.

The boys scattered. One ran into the garage and came back with a piece of pipe. William ran into the bedroom. He came out with a coat hanger. The two boys signaled to each other, then silently crept up behind the old couple and strangled them to death with a pipe and a coat hanger.

All they wanted was a little excitement and a little pocket change. Murder was not in their plans when they went riding that night, but murder was never far from their minds. They were already desensitized from hours of horrific killing in video games and movies. With that kind of desensitization, a mass of flesh with a beating heart, air filled lungs, a plethora of human emotions and a loving family, becomes a mere object. When an object is in your way, you simply move it. That's all they really did. They moved some objects out of their way, found some money and other items they wanted and left for the video arcade.

If a piece of pipe and a coat hanger can readily become lethal weapons, what is the purpose of focusing all of our attention on guns? Certainly guns are used all too often in murders, but what about knives, kitchen knives?

The stories are very gruesome, but suffice it to say, murder with kitchen knives is quite common. How will we rid ourselves of all those kitchen knives?

I have never had a weapon and I never intend to have one. Once, a co-worker brought a gun into my car to travel about ninety minutes down the highway to a workshop. I said, "What are you doing? I won't have that thing in my car. If you need a gun, you'll have to go in another car."

Shocked at my reaction, she asked nervously, "What if something happens on the road?"

Firmly, I responded, "I have a weapon a whole lot more powerful than that one, so I'm really not worried." (Psalm. 124:8; Isaiah. 54:17)

With this perspective on weapons, I am certainly not an advocate of every house in America being armed. However, I just know from experience that the National Rifle Association propaganda is correct. "Guns don't kill people, people do." However, I would amend that propaganda to say, "Guns don't kill people, *desensitized* people do." If children are to remain safely sensitive individuals, hold deeply caring relationships and honor for life itself, what parents must guard against is desensitization.

Life Defining Scars

Let no corrupt communication proceed out of your mouth, but that which is good to the use of edifying that it may minister grace unto the hearers. — Ephesians 4:29

R ule of Thumb: However long it took to create the problem, it will take at least that long or longer to resolve it.

The longer we allow any problem to grow, the longer it will take to resolve it once we make a decision for resolution. Therefore, once a problem is recognized, it is destructive to dwell on who caused the problem and waste time placing blame, as the problem only grows larger. Take action as quickly as possible to remedy the situation, before it grows to greater, more harmful proportions.

Before going any further, let's take a moment to face a devastating reality. Some problems cannot be fixed by human intervention. It is a hard, cold fact: Despite our best intentions and our best efforts to gather the best tools for our Parenting Business, our child may not respond! I have said it before and will probably say it many times again: When problems seem insurmountable, turning to prayer and having faith that God will resolve the problem if we give it to Him, and leave it with Him, is the best tool any parent can have in their Parenting Business toolbox!

As my children have become adults, they have taken paths of their own choosing. Short of telling them they can or cannot come to visit me, I no longer have any control over their daily comings and goings. More importantly, I have absolutely no control over the decisions they make for their lives. I also have no control over how they interpret their childhood experiences and apply those perceptions to their decisions. They are adults now, and responsible for their own choices. While I eagerly remain readily available to them, if they choose to ask me for help, I can only pray that they will be blessed and protected and make good decisions for their lives.

I'm not sure why we typically say, "We can *only* pray." Prayer is the most powerful tool we have; not the last resort. In fact, it should be the first resort, whether we are faced with a dilemma or not. Saying it is the "only" thing we can do, diminishes the importance of the power of prayer. Again, I have no idea of the workings of the supernatural power of God, I only know that as He promised, He answers prayer, every time. Sometimes we may not think prayer is working, because answers are not forthcoming immediately, or as quickly as we would like. However, answers are forthcoming in God's perfect timing. We must muster the faith to believe that is true. For me, the hardest part of maintaining faith is coming to grips with the fact that sometimes God's answer to prayer is, "No."

The reality is that you may work diligently to develop the most excellent parenting skills, and they just don't work! Sometimes those skills will work for one child, but not another. It remains a mystery as to why two children born to the same parents, living in the same household and having virtually the same life experiences, will react differently to the same event. This is a mystery that may never be resolved. However, when all you know and all you have learned does not seem to be working, you still have several viable options remaining:

1) Pray and continue to pray, *believing* that God is in total control of the situation and you are only one of the vessels He will use to accomplish His plan. (Psalm 17:6; Matthew 7:7-8; 8:13; 21:22)

2) Continue to seek new parenting tools. One you haven't found yet may just work!

3) Accept the reality that your child has a mind and spirit all his own, and he just may not make the choices you want him to make.

4) Continue to be an AHHBUT parent, recognizing that while a tool may not work right now, it may work in the future.

5) Keep praying and believing.

It is simply impossible for anyone to go through life without suffering painful experiences. It is even more impossible to parent a child without making some of the very mistakes that cause pain to that child. After appropriate apologies have been made, it benefits no one to waste time dwelling on the mistake or stewing over a guilty conscience. Matthew 6:27 says, "Which of you by taking thought can add one cubit unto his stature?" The fact is; this is not the only painful encounter your child will experience in life. Sadly, it is unlikely it will be the only painful encounter your child will experience at your very own hand.

Once your child is wounded, all you can do is assume your full responsibility as CEO of your Parenting Business, sincerely apologize and begin to sooth your child's pain the best way you know how. Occasionally that means stepping in and taking some concrete action. Sometimes it means talking your heart out. At other times it means just sitting there and listening, silently.

Each event we experience in life becomes part of our own interpretation of who we are—our self-identity. The way we incorporate life's hurtful experiences into our definition of who we are, determines whether those experiences will create character lines or ugly scars.

If we could but anticipate all of the damaging experiences our children might encounter throughout life, by our own hand or the hands of others, we could take steps to assure they would avoid those ugly scars and defacing blemishes. We look at a newborn baby and marvel at his perfection. We say, "I wish he could stay this way forever." We want so much to keep the baby from experiencing the pain we know is out there, lurking, waiting to begin etching painful, ugly marks into this tiny object of perfection. But, it is not going to happen. As the baby grows, so do the life experiences that begin to form his or her character; all of those same experiences we prayed could be avoided. Some of those experiences create life-defining scars.

What are some experiences encountered on the highway of life that would cause such scars?

Scarring experiences in life come from many directions. Some of them you will never know.

First, it is humanly impossible to be with your children twenty-four hours a day, every day of their lives. Therefore, it may be a baby-sitter, a relative, another child, the postman, a neighbor, the storekeeper, the doctor or nurse, the auto mechanic, a vagrant on the street, the day care worker, a teacher, a person in the clergy-—and yes, even a character in a movie or television show. Heaven only knows who might say one unkind word, make one searing comment, give one hateful gesture, or one disapproving glance, to touch something in the heart of your child in the wrong way.

Second, when your child has such an encounter, he may never mention it to you. Being so uncomfortable with the feelings elicited from the experience, he may well believe he is the one at fault. Believing he must have done something wrong—because an all-knowing and certainly all-powerful adult or a more popular and more confident-appearing peer would never have said or done such a hurtful thing—your child may never mention the experience. He may bury the resulting pain alive within himself, creating a life-defining scar.

Because young children experience life very literally, comments made to them are absorbed quite differently than when similar comments are made to an adolescent or adult.

I remember clearly the day my mother made the one comment that dramatically defined the course of my own life. She was taking me with her in the car to pick up my father at work. I was barely five, and even now I remember the comment as though it were yesterday. It was a comment I buried deep inside for almost forty years. It was a comment that clearly directed the path of my life.

My father worked at my grandparents' glass company, located at the edge of a dingy downtown area just alongside the railroad tracks of a mid-sized community in the North. Directly across the tracks from my grandparents' store, stood a huge, dark red brick building with rows of windows uniformly spaced across the building from the bottom to the top.

As we sat at the red light in silence, my mother suddenly pointed to the building and mused out loud, "It is such a tragedy. Those people in that tenement are so poor they have to sew their children's underwear onto their bodies in the winter, to keep them from freezing to death."

The light changed and we turned the corner to pick up my father.

I felt the piercing pain of needles in my skin, as I literally interpreted the comment. I wrapped my arms tightly around my waist, hugging away my own pain. How else was I to interpret that statement? I was five years old and had already learned somewhere, not to share scary thoughts and feelings with my mother. In fact, I never mentioned the comment, let alone the fear and pain it evoked, to anyone. The feelings were foreign to me—they scared me! I wondered why my mother appeared to be unconcerned by the thought of needles piercing the skin of innocent children. Perhaps I wasn't supposed to feel this "strange" way. Perhaps there was something wrong with me that I was experiencing these terribly uncomfortable feelings. If it was such a tragedy, why wasn't she running into the building and soothing the pain of all those children? Was she heartless? I buried my thoughts and fears, and even terror, deep within myself, never speaking of it.

I have no idea how often or how long I vividly reflected on that statement. I buried it. In fact, before I realized it, I was in my forties and working at a maximum-security juvenile facility in Texas. One winter afternoon a group of colleagues was chatting, when a one of them, who was originally from "up North" commented, "I can't believe you guys really think this is cold weather. You have no idea what cold is, until you spend the winter up North. Up there it gets so cold people actually have to keep their children warm by sewing their underwear on them."

If someone had thrown ice water in my face in the dead of winter, I couldn't have been more stunned! The buried experience and its accompanying fears rushed forth from my memory bank, and this time I understood what that statement really meant! This time, there were no needles piercing my skin. There were no foreign feelings evoked by that comment. As an adult now, I understood the meaning of that life defining statement I had buried deep within myself for forty years.

At that moment I realized the reason I yearned to help others less fortunate than myself. There was a certain irony in learning that my mother, who had a significant disdain for social workers, actually made the one life-defining comment that sent me on a quest to be a social worker— when I was only five years old. I always had a deep concern for people who were "suffering," just as I imagined those poor children were suffering as clothes were sewn to their bodies. Indeed, that single unintentionally painful, virtually insignificant, deeply sensitive remark became a life-defining scar that set me on the path my life would take. It only took one comment to define the course of my life.

Even when a comment is well intended or compassionate, as I imagine my mother's comment had been, it may have irreversible consequences—good or bad. The saying on my calendar this month is: *"Water and words are easy to pour, but impossible to recover."* Words are powerful. We must be responsible with them.

When Words Scar

...the God of all comfort; who comforteth us in all our tribulation, that we may be able to comfort them which are in any trouble, by the comfort wherewith we ourselves are comforted of God. — *II Corinthians 1:3–4*

The deepest wounds experienced in life are most often the result of unkind words being hurled through space without thought or care about how their impact will affect the recipient. There are simply some truths in life that are inescapable. For example, it is almost inhuman to have never hurled unkind words. It is just as inhuman to have never been the recipient of unkind words. While, as the recipient we have a choice of how we will interpret those piercing words, when unkind words are hurled through space and land, they create scars. All too often those scars are life-defining.

EXAMPLES OF TYPICAL INSENSITIVE COMMENTS
POTENTIALLY CREATING LIFE-DEFINING SCARS

COMMENT AND/OR BEHAVIOR OBSERVED BY CHILD	CHILD'S POSSIBLE INTERNALIZATION OF OBSERVED COMMENT/BEHAVIOR
"It's nasty to spit out your food."	"I'm nasty."
"Stand still. You're going to break something." Returns to shopping.	"He/she doesn't trust me; doesn't even like being with me. I'm not likeable."
"Not now!" Turning and walking away.	"I'm nothing but trouble."

Comment and/or Behavior Observed By Child	Child's Possible Internalization of Observed Comment/Behavior
"Big boys/girls don't cry. Stop acting like a baby."	"I better keep my feelings to myself."
"You little brat." Disgusted expression.	"I'm worthless."
"I don't want to hear it." Back to reading the paper.	"I need to keep my thoughts to myself."
"Get out of here." "Don't bother me. Can't you see I'm on the phone?" Returns to phone conversation.	"I'm just one big bother."
"Can't you do anything right? Here, let me do it." Taking the project away from the child.	"I'm stupid. "
"Skinny-Minnie;" "Lard-O;" "Baby;" "Stinky;" "Frizzle Hair;" "Dumbo;" "Snaggle Tooth;" "Pervert" "Nerd," Etc.	"There's something wrong with me." "I'm just one big loser."
"Are you stupid or something?"	"I am worthless."
"I can't wait until you can drive. I'm tired of carpooling you everywhere." Grabbing the keys & slamming the door on the way to the car.	"You want me out of your way. Believe me, I'll get out of your way! When I can drive, you'll never see my face again. "

It does not take all of these comments, or comments like them, from any one particular person, to create a life-defining scar. Certainly, repetitive experiences with bullies or insensitive adults can push a child over the threshold. However, sometimes it only takes one comment, insensitive or not—intentional or not.

If you were to imagine taking a clean piece of paper and crumpling it into a tight ball and then opening it flat again, you would probably envision a wide variety of furrows and wrinkles defining what was once a smooth piece of paper. If you then were to imagine taking your fingers and gently smoothing those defining lines, you would probably imagine that the more you rub the paper, the smoother the lines and wrinkles will appear, although they are still visible.

In "real life" each time we experience a painful encounter, a scar appears within. If you looked at your formerly crumpled, but now smoothed paper, you would notice that some "scars" are deeper and more defined than others. So it is with hurtful life experiences. Some scars actually furrow so deeply that they come to define our personal values and beliefs about ourselves. Those are usually scars from the repetition of the same type of hurtful experiences or from a singular, excruciating experience. While those scars become our definition of who we are, other scars make us more cautious. Those may be scars from occasional or one-time gravely painful experiences. Some scars are barely visible. We hardly remember them. Those are probably scars from the routine bumps and bruises of every day life that serve as reminders of how we can avoid future harm.

That piece of paper represents you. It represents your children. That piece of paper represents the imperfections in all people. No matter how much good happens to smooth the scars, they are still there. They may become less severe, or become less noticeable. We may think about them less and less as time moves on and as we have more positive experiences, however, they are still there—-those scars form our "fragile identity." We base our choices on just how fragile those scars are. Like a scab covered wound, they remain dormant, yet ready and waiting to become a gaping wound again, if pricked.

As a diligent CEO of your Parenting Business, it is your responsibility to be watchful. Not only must you be watchful of the words you use, but you must also be watchful of how your children interpret your words and the words of others.

Safely Sharing The World With Isolating Children

He shall feed his flock like a shepherd: He shall gather the lambs with his arm, and carry them in his bosom, and shall gently lead those that are with young. — Isaiah 40:11

In the writings of Haim Ginot, a highly acclaimed Israeli author of parenting books back in the seventies, he commented that it is highly unlikely that any parent wakes up each morning plotting ways to make their child's life miserable—but they do!

It is highly unlikely that any mistake you make in parenting your child is intentional. However, once the "horse is out of the barn," what can you do? **You can become fully available and accessible to your child!**

After your child experiences a difficult encounter with you (or anyone else, for that matter), you must make yourself available to observe for signs that your child may have been wounded emotionally and is forming a scar. Because you may not be aware that your child has been wounded, you must be vigilant to observe for signs that he is hurting. A most typical sign is isolation. Unfortunately, isolation is not always visible.

When stressed, all of us isolate to some degree. This does not necessarily mean we rush to the bedroom, slam the door, slap on a set of earphones and blast music into our ears to block out the world, although this is clearly a sign of isolation. More often isolation is much more subtle.

Each of us has found our self in a room full of people, not hearing a word being said. That is the most dangerous form of isolation. From all outward appearances we seem to be functioning normally, but on the inside we may be experiencing anguish that no one can see. This is exactly the moment that destructive, even evil, plots are prone to begin in our mind!

Isolation in its most positive form is a self-protective defense mechanism, which if taken too far, can become destructive. When we are overloaded and just cannot absorb any more stimuli or do not have sufficient energy to deal with certain information, an internal switch says "no more," and we shut down to the outside world. However, if we are troubled and do not allow others to see our pain, no one can help us resolve it. As adults, we may (and I emphasize "may") have developed the internal resources to work through our problems alone. However, children clearly have not developed sufficient internal resources to resolve their problems appropriately, without some outside help. The problem is, very often they won't let us see their problems. It is very difficult to help when you can't see the problem!

Children are quite adept at isolating in plain sight! They might be watching TV or playing hopscotch or clicking away on the computer and look just fine, but their minds may be miles away. The easiest way to learn whether your child is truly involved in the activity or not, is to show some genuine interest in what you see him doing. Ask him a legitimate question about it. If he seems to respond clearly, logically, rationally and without hesitation, he is probably fine. However, if he remains silent, sullen, angry, irritated or even annoyed, there is reason for concern. There is even greater concern if he stumbles over his words and seems to have to gather his thoughts before making a logical statement or, cannot give you an answer at all. These responses, or "non-responses" are strong indications that he may be, and probably is, isolating.

Don't panic! Simply stick around long enough to develop a conversation. If he looks sad or upset, say so and build on his response to get that conversation going—even if his response is only, "Yeah." Be prepared to spend some time—a lot of time. Most often there is no short cut to determining whether your child is isolating or not. It often takes significant perseverance and patience to convince an isolated person to come into the light.

I don't know what compelled me to do it, the day I planted myself on the end of Kayla's bed and informed her that I refused to move until she told me what was bothering her. She was about fifteen, and walked right past me when she came home from school that day, without so much as a "Hello." While we had our problems as mother and daughter, she generally acknowledged my presence.

Feeling somewhat slighted by her dismissal of me, I stood in the hallway for several minutes after she had gone to her bedroom and shut the door. I just knew this was not typical behavior for her. I searched myself to recall whether I had done something that might have upset her. The list was growing in my mind, although none of the incidents I recalled had occurred within the past twenty-four hours. Since I had not noticed this aloof behavior when she left for school in the morning, I could only conclude that something had happened during the day. Although, I was busy preparing dinner at the time of this incident, I made a difficult decision. I decided to turn off the stove and take the time to learn why Kayla was isolating herself.

I knocked on her bedroom door. She did not respond. I knocked again. When she still did not respond, I cracked the door and peeked in to find her curled up in a ball on her bed with her face smashed into the pillow. I asked, "What's the matter?"

"Nothing," was her muffled response.

"It looks like something," I countered.

"Nothing," she mumbled into her pillow.

"You just look so sad," I noted.

"Go away," was her response.

I sat down on the end of her bed and said, "I'd really like to know what the problem is."

"Go away!" she retorted.

"No. I'm not going to leave you alone until you tell me what's wrong. I'm going to sit right here if it takes all night!"

I almost wanted to eat those words as thirty minutes turned into an hour and an hour became two, before she suddenly sat up on her bed and shouted, "Why won't you go away?"

"Because I care about you and want to help you feel better," I replied.

"There's nothing you can do!" she yelled.

"I can listen," I said as calmly as possible.

"It's got nothing to do with you," she insisted.

"Yes it does, anything that happens to you, has to do with me. I love you. When you love someone, anything that hurts them, hurts you. So this has everything to do with me."

"Tommy broke up with me," she blurted tearfully.

"I am so sorry." I said simply, as I gathered her in my arms and held her while she sobbed her heart out.

I don't think I said much more during that encounter. Sometimes it just hurts too much to talk. While she was still saddened by the demise of her teenage romance, she would talk to me about it occasionally when the feelings started to resurface, releasing her anguish in bits and pieces.

Quite likely, she would have worked through this teenage tragedy and moved on to other relationships without my planting myself on the foot of her bed. However, a more dangerous outcome is also a possibility.

Mrs. Stockton described her daughter Brenda as an active, outgoing young lady. She described how Brenda especially enjoyed working with underprivileged children. According to Mrs. Stockton, Brenda had received a number of awards for her volunteer work. She seemed to have a passion for helping others, less fortunate than herself.

In her senior year of high school, Brenda began making plans for college. She was excited to be heading off to live in a dorm and become more independent. Eddie, her boyfriend of the last three years, would be attending the same university and living in a nearby dorm. They seemed rather mature about their relationship, saying they wanted to get a year or two of college under their belts before totally committing to their relationship. Both Mr. and Mrs. Stockton were happy they had made this decision. While they liked Eddie, they felt Brenda needed an opportunity to meet some new people, including potential new boyfriends.

Toward the end of the school year, Mrs. Stockton took Brenda to shop for her prom dress. As Brenda twirled around showing off a dress she particularly liked, Mrs. Stockton noticed what appeared to be a fading bruise on her shoulder. As she reflected on what she saw, she said it looked a bit like a handprint. She started to say something, but Brenda seemed so excited that she did not want to put a damper on

*the occasion. Brenda selected that dress and they happily left the store
to look for matching shoes.*

*A couple of weeks later Mrs. Stockton thought she noted a small
cluster of bruises on Brenda's neck. They looked like fingerprints. However, she was busy that evening completing the paper work to close a
real estate sale the next day, and she did not have a chance to check
out what she saw. She said that she had truly forgotten the incident by
the time she saw Brenda the next morning.*

*Just before the prom, Mrs. Stockton noted that Brenda was un-
commonly quiet and seemed to be spending more time in her room
than usual. She recalled her own anxiety about high school gradua-
tion and deduced that Brenda was getting anxious about the ending
of high school and the beginning of a virtually new life as a college
freshman. She made a few comments to Brenda to let her know that
college would be fun, but she did not take the time to really sit down
and talk to her.*

*Then, on prom night Mrs. Stockton noted that Brenda seemed
much less exuberant than she had expected her to be on such an important occasion. She did ask Brenda what was wrong, and Brenda
answered that she didn't feel well. Mrs. Stockton said something to the
effect that it was a shame Brenda wasn't feeling well on such an important evening and asked if she could get something for her stomach.
Brenda said, "No."*

*She knew that Brenda would be out late that night, but began
worrying when two-thirty A.M. rolled around, and Brenda was not
home. At three o'clock she began looking out the window incessantly.
At three-thirty she woke her husband, who acknowledged it was late,
but assumed the kids were just celebrating. Mrs. Stockton said she did
not sleep the rest of the night, and by the time the sun came up she
knew deep in her heart that celebrating was not the reason Brenda
had not come home.*

*It was almost a month before a couple of young boys chasing squir-
rels with their pellet guns stumbled over Brenda's body where it lay
decomposing in a vacant field.*

*The Stockton's went to the police station to learn the results of the
autopsy. The autopsy results indicated that Brenda had been beaten
and strangled to death. On the way home, twelve-year-old Missy and*

fifteen-year-old Andrew cried their hearts out, asking questions about
who could have done such a terrible thing to their sister. Sammy, Bren-
da's thirteen-year-old brother sat in stoic silence.

The moment the family returned home, Sammy grabbed his base-
ball bat and walked out of the house. The Stockton's thought it was
a good thing he was going to take his anguish out on a baseball, and
said nothing. However, Sammy did not take a ball to bat around. In-
stead, he went in search of Brenda's boyfriend, Eddie, and when he
found him, began swinging the baseball bat with all his might, causing
severe and permanent brain damage. Eddie remained in a coma and
on a respirator for several weeks before he died. Then, the attempted
murder charges against Sammy were changed to murder.

When we isolate, we have no outlet for our feelings, stuffing them
away deep inside ourselves. The more we stuff our hurts, the more we
hurt. When we hurt badly enough and cannot, or will not, expel the
pain with words, we act out that hurt in some form of rage toward
others or ourselves. Just like sweeping dirt under the rug, it eventually spills out somewhere, and it's not a pretty sight.

Isolation is often impossible to see. Although your child may
become less talkative or spend much time alone, isolation is more
likely to be felt, than seen. When you sense your child is isolating,
you must make yourself fully available to keep your eyes and ears
open for clues that an issue may be festering. If you sense even a
hint that your child is detaching, withdrawing into himself, talk to
him about it. Simply say, with genuine sincerity and a willingness
to be engaged for an hour or more, "It seems like something may be
bothering you. Whatever it is, I'd sure like to help you work it out."
Whether there is a problem or not, he is likely to deny it. Beware of
accepting that denial because it's easier for you. Unless you are fully
satisfied with the denial, continue to dig for more information until
you are fully satisfied.

One hint on digging: Be vigilant. You may have noted that when
I became concerned that Kayla was isolating, my first approach was
to ask her an almost accusatory question; "What's the matter?" as
though she must have done something wrong, herself. You will also
notice that the response I received was totally unproductive; "Nothing." However, once I began making less threatening comments in

the form of observations about her demeanor, the responses eventually became more productive.

We have all done it. Your friend smashes a finger in the car door, and you wince in sympathetic pain as you ask, "Are you okay?" almost as if willing him to be okay, and thereby denying him his pain! You know he's not okay, however despite unbearable, throbbing pain, he most likely responds, "Sure, I'm fine. It's nothing." However, if someone happens to pop into the conversation and comment, "Wow! I bet that hurts," acknowledging the pain, despite the initial denial, your friend most likely will now admit, "You better believe it hurts!!! It hurts like heck!!!" The acknowledgement of his pain seems to give him the freedom to admit it. The same is true when your child is isolating in internal pain.

With a good deal of sensitivity and a lot of prayer and patience, you can pursue the concern quietly and calmly, until you are fully satisfied that the problem has been revealed, adequately examined, and is on the road to resolution, or that there really is no problem. Only by openly talking about it, will you ever know if there is a legitimate problem or not.

Most often, when you experience that little nagging feeling that something is out of sorts, you are right! When you feel that something is just not right, always check it out. Isolation may be hard to see, but when it turns to anger it will be more visible and also more dangerous.

EXAMPLES FOR *GETTING STARTED IN* CHECKING OUT POSSIBLE ISOLATION

The following scenarios may help you begin uncovering the possibility that your child may be isolating. Be aware, these examples are *only a starting* place. You must commit to spend some time digging. While there are only two suggested checks noted in each of these examples, it may take **many** more checks to determine whether there is a serious problem. *Keep checking* until you feel truly satisfied that there is no problem, or until the real problem surfaces and you can talk about it openly.

Situation	1st Isolation Check	Child's Response	2nd Isolation Re-check
You notice that your child has not asked to go to his best friend's house for several days.	"I noticed you haven't gone to Bobby's for a couple days."	"Uh huh."	"You used to be together after school almost every day."
Your child seems distant, but you can't put you finger on it.	"I feel like you're not yourself lately."	"Why?"	"It just seems that something might be bothering you."
Your child generally has a hearty appetite, but has not been eating breakfast and picks at his food at meals.	"It looks like you don't have much of an appetite lately."	"I'm not hungry."	"I wonder if you're getting the flu, or maybe have something on your mind that's bothering you."
Your child constantly has earphones blasting music in his ears. You have to yell to be heard.	"I know you love your music, but I'd like to just talk to you sometime."	"I want to listen to this tape."	"Let's listen to the tape together on the stereo. Or, maybe you just don't feel like talking?"
Your child seems to be using friends, school and other activities as excuses to stay away from home.	"You sure have been busy lately."	"You're busy all the time too."	"I'm sorry it seems like that. What could we do to have more time for each other?"

Situation	1st Isolation Check	Child's Response	2nd Isolation Re-check
Your child spends most of his time in his room, when he's at home.	"It seems like you're spending a lot of time in your room."	"So what? It's my room."	"I know you like your privacy, but was just hoping we could spend some time together."
Your child sits in the room with the family, but rarely says a word.	"Tommy, it seems like you're mighty quiet to-night."	"Get off my case."	"You just seem really quiet. If I had to guess, I'd say something's troubling you."
Your child's be-loved aunt died and your child seems to be tak-ing it very well.	"I know you loved your aunt. I'm sure you're really sad she's gone."	"Yeah."	"It's going to be hard not having her to talk to, isn't it?"

Safely Sharing The World With Angry Children

A soft answer turneth away wrath; but grievous words stir up anger. — *Proverbs 15:1*

When we sit in isolation, stewing over a problem, we usually begin to feel powerless to do anything about that problem and become angry at our helplessness. With anger, the problem becomes more visible. Anger is much easier to recognize than isolation—voices raise, doors slam, objects are hurled through the air! Even when it's silent, anger is visible. While anger is often a healthy and appropriate emotion, left unchecked, it can also become fertile ground for danger. The plot for destruction may thicken.

When your child is showing clear signs of anger, you must talk about it with him. This is especially important when the encounter resulting in the anger has been with you. You must first assess your own feelings about the incident. It is best to wait until you resolve your own frayed feelings, before attempting to negotiate a remedy to the problem. Confronting such an encounter while you are in the heat of anger, will likely serve only to intensify the problem! However, failure to address the concern at all only pushes it underground—it does not disappear, but becomes rooted as an internal scar, which if pricked, may become an internal gaping wound. The deeper the underground anger and unforgiveness, the more fragile the identity issues will become.

Shouldn't I just wait until my child says something?

Absolutely not!

When we see no obvious signs of anger or unforgiveness, we are all too happy to let the issue slide. No one enjoys engaging in conversations about uncomfortable issues. Therefore, we are at risk of making ourselves believe that the problem is resolved. We may think about it occasionally, pushing it away with the thought that our child has never mentioned it, so he must have forgotten the incident. We distract ourselves with the concern that bringing up the topic will only be a reminder of a painful experience. Initially, this may seem like the easiest solution. However, in the long run, as the problem goes underground and becomes rooted as an internal scar, avoiding the issue will result in even bigger problems.

Any experience—good or bad, remains an integral part of our identity. There is no escaping that fact. Therefore, it is always beneficial to regularly check the status of the experience. When it comes to your mind, check it out with your child. If it truly is not a problem, bringing it up will cause no harm and it is most likely that your child will interpret your effort as an act of caring and love. Thus, when a real problem arises, he will be more accepting of your efforts to help. However, if it remains a problem, bringing it up offers you a new opportunity to help your child resolve the issue. As with isolating, there is no quick fix for anger; when you open the door, plan to stay awhile.

EXAMPLE: DETERMINING WHETHER YOUR CHILD IS ISOLATING AND POSSIBLY ANGRY.

Problem: Parent realizes he hasn't spent much time with his child in a long, long time and wants to try to remedy the situation by having a friendly chat. When the parent hears himself doing all of the talking, he suddenly realizes the child may be isolating and his isolation has probably already grown into anger. The parent knows this is going to take a long time, and prepares to give his child all the time he needs to work out the problem.

Parent: "Hey son! That looks like an interesting TV show. Can I watch with you?

Child: "Uh huh."

Parent	Takes a seat in a nearby chair. "Catch me up on the plot."
Child:	Slumps down further on the couch. "It's about this guy."
Parent:	"So, what's this guy up to?"
Child:	"I dunno."
Parent:	"Well, the show's been on almost thirty minutes. What's happened?"
Child:	"I dunno."
Parent:	Leans forward to express genuine concern. "It sounds like your mind is on something else besides the TV show."
Child:	"Not really."
Parent:	"You sound like you're not really interested in this TV show, so I'm wondering why you haven't changed channels. We can watch something else if you want. Why don't you go ahead and change channels?"
Child:	Mumbling, "Just too tired."
Parent:	"Well, you've got the remote right there. Do you want to check out what else is on?"
Child:	"No."
Parent:	"Generally when someone's got the remote right next to them and they don't change channels, it means they're pretty interested in what's on."
Child:	Silence
Parent:	"Or, of course it could mean their mind isn't on the TV show."
Child:	Silence
Parent:	"You seem really quiet."
Child:	"Don't feel like talking."
Parent:	"Well, it seems like maybe something's bothering you."
Child:	Raising his voice, "I said I don't feel like talking."
Parent:	Remaining calm and committed, "I sure don't want you to think you have to go this alone—whatever it is."
Child:	"Why all these questions? You never wanted to talk before."

Parent:	"You know—you're right. I haven't been talking with you much. In fact, I've been thinking about that a lot lately. I'd sure like to change that."
Child:	Starts to stand up. "I'm going to my room."
Parent:	"I'd really like it if we could talk about this."
Child:	Fully standing now. "Whatcha' gonna do? Follow me to my room?"
Parent:	"Maybe."
Child:	Walking toward his room. "Well, don't! You don't have to know everything about my life."
Parent:	Stands up and begins to follow his child into the bedroom. "I realize I haven't been involved in your life for far too long. I'm really sorry about that. I'd really like to change it, if you'll let me. Like right now, when something's bothering you, I'd sure like to help you with it."
Child:	Turns to block the doorway to his bedroom. "Maybe it's just too late."
Parent:	Remaining calm, "Are you saying it's too late for us to build our relationship, or it's too late to help you with your problem?"
Child:	Really angry and yelling now, "I'm saying you weren't there when I needed you, so it's too late to start now."
Parent:	With genuine humility, "I really feel terrible about that. You're absolutely right about my not being there before, but I don't agree that it's too late for us to start trying to make things better."
Child:	Defiantly, "Well, now I don't want a relationship with you."
Parent:	"I'm really sorry to hear you say that. What can I do to change your mind?"
Child:	"Nothing."
Parent:	"Then, all I can do is tell you I'm sorry and want to change things between us. I can't make you accept that."
Child:	"No you can't."
Parent:	"I can only tell you again that I'm sorry and make

	a commitment to give more attention to our relationship, if you'll give it another chance."
Child:	"How do I know you mean what you say?"
Parent:	"Well, I guess you don't. I can only tell you what's on my heart right now, and hope you'll give us another chance.
Child:	"It would take a whole lot for me to trust you again."
Parent:	"I'm sure it would, but I can't show you I mean what I say, if you won't let me."
Child:	"If I did let you, it's not going to be anything big. Like I'm not going to put my neck out there and have you not show up again."
Parent:	Sincerely, "I can't promise you I'll be perfect, but I sure can guarantee you I'll give it my best shot, if you'll give it a try."
Child:	"Well, Tommy's father takes him fishing and hunting and sometimes bowling. How come you don't do that stuff with me?"
Parent:	"I'd like us to do things together."
Child:	Still angry, "You say that, but I don't believe you. We used to do things together when I was a kid, but it all stopped. Why?"
Parent:	"I'm not exactly sure. I think I just got my priorities all mixed up and started spending more time working, when I should have been spending time with the family. Now I can see where that was really wrong. I'd like to change that."
Child:	"Well, if you want to change it, you have to prove it."
Parent:	"I'm not sure how I can prove it. Can you think of a way?"
Child:	"Well, maybe if we do something I like to do, even if you don't. "
Parent:	"Under the circumstances, I think that's only fair. Where can we start?"
Child:	With caution, "Take me to the monster truck show Saturday."

Parent: Swallowing distaste for the particular event, "Monster trucks, huh? If you're willing to give this a shot, I can sure meet you half way. Monster trucks, it is! Well, let's do it! I'll get tickets and we'll go."

It may take a great deal of patience and even more humility to make inroads when our child is hurting—especially when our child is hurting because of something we have done. A less committed parent might have handled the situation much differently—and much less effectively.

EXAMPLE: PARENT WOULD LIKE A BETTER RELATIONSHIP WITH HIS CHILD, BUT HAS A VERY DIFFERENT ATTITUDE.

Parent: "Hey son, what are you watching?"
Child: "Just some show."
Parent: "Can I watch with you?"
Child: Mumbling, "Do what you want—you always do."
Parent: Getting defensive, "Geez, I come in here to spend some time with you and I get your same old attitude."
Child: Gets up and goes to his bedroom.
Parent: Thinking to himself, "That's the thanks I get for trying to be involved in his life. Forget it. I've got better things to do with my time."

With an attitude like that, the problem will never be resolved. In fact, the child's anger will only grow to more dangerous proportions.

Listen!

He that hath knowledge spareth his words; and a man of understanding is of an excellent spirit. —Proverbs 17:27

We hear it all of the time. "Talk to your children." I disagree.

It will better serve us to say, "**Listen** to your children." Productive communication is more about listening than talking.

Many people believe the adult must do all of the talking, giving information, never receiving it, especially when a child is involved. In some cases adults believe it is rude for a child to give information to an adult. It is "back-talk." In other cases adults believe it weakens their authority to seek or accept information from a child. The child may begin to believe he now has more power than the adult!

I disagree with that, also.

～

Children provide bright, fresh, creative ideas—a new perspective on things. More importantly, they hold the key to what makes them tick! We can learn much from listening to a child. We can especially learn much **about that child,** by listening to him. However, before you can listen to a child and truly hear what is being said, you must truly believe it is the right thing to do.

As a new employee at the juvenile facility, I sometimes found myself with a youth when circumstances required information about campus procedures. When no adult was available, it seemed logical to me to ask for directions from the one person with me—the youth!

The first youth from the school that I requested to come to my office appeared and handed me a slip of paper, which I promptly lost in a mass of other papers accumulating on my desk. When our session ended, I expected he would return to the campus school. Instead, he stood silently by my desk. I asked if he needed something more. He then informed me there was a procedure for youth walking between buildings. I asked what that procedure was, and he gave me a detailed explanation, which then required my hunting for that lost piece of paper on my desk.

If I happened to mention to another staff member that I received my information from a youth, they would invariably say, "Never listen to anything these kids have to say. They are going to mislead you, and you are either going to get hurt or get in trouble."

It never happened. My response to these comments became, "Oh! Is the information he gave me, incorrect?"

"Well, no. It's just that you don't want to give them the upper hand. You'll look weak and they'll take advantage of you if they think you don't know what to do."

I know I am blessed. I spent much time alone with these youth, even walking across the large campus in the dark of night with a group of juvenile offenders. They never misled me. They never hurt me. They never even tried.

Of course, I prayed for safety, theirs and mine. I believe that what I heard as an answer to prayer was: "You will get what you expect—expect the best!" Indeed, the Bible tells us that if we ask, believing, we will receive what we ask. (Matthew 21:22)

Among professional counselors there is a firm belief that one gets what they expect. It is called a "self-fulfilling prophesy." Perhaps you will recall this notable experiment from many years ago. At the beginning of a school year teachers were specifically given the names of students whose prior records indicated them to be high achievers, as well as the names of those students who were failures. Indeed, by the end of the school year, the teachers found the information to be correct. Those students reported to be failures, failed. Those students reported to be high achievers, did well. However, what the teachers did not know was that the names of the children in each category had been randomly selected and were not at all factual. Indeed, the teachers got exactly the performances they expected.

When we expect the best from children, we usually receive it. When we expect the worst from children, we generally receive that, too. Therefore, if we expect and really desire children to communicate with us appropriately, we must believe they can and will.

"Communicate with a baby?" "Communicate with a three year old?" Better yet, "Communicate with a teenager?"

Absolutely! My years of working in adoption counseling taught me well about the critical importance of maintaining open lines of communication with all children, from their earliest days.

In years past, it was standard procedure to keep adoption issues "secret," especially from the adopted child. The child "shouldn't be told." If the child were told anything about the adoption, it needed to be "at an age when they can understand." Then, if they ever reached that magical age of understanding, they were only to be told half-truths. For example: There had been a birth mother (true)—all birth mothers were fairy princesses or at least college cheerleaders (untrue). There had been a birth father (true)—all birth fathers were gallant princes, or at least quarterbacks of their college football teams (untrue).

As time passed, doors began to open in adoption. Of all things, adoptees were learning they were adopted! Some learned at fifty or sixty years of age or older, when going through documents upon the death of their parents, they found their own adoption records. They became angry about being lied to (often by omission) all of those years. Essentially, their whole life had been based on a lie. It became very clear that attempts to build relationships on lies, half-truths and silences placed relationships on very shaky ground.

As the number of distraught adoptees mounted, professionals in the field of adoption agreed with them, that there was no age too early to begin talking with a child about his adoption. We advised parents to begin using the word "adoption" from the moment they took a baby into their family. We suggested holding and rocking the baby while telling him, "How wonderful it is to have 'adopted' you."

Words can be frightening, especially unfamiliar words. How often have you heard that a child has asked, "What does 'adoption' mean, Mommy?" How often have you heard similar questions asked of parents about various complex and difficult issues? In the speeding world we live in, issues such as prejudice, divorce, sexuality, drugs, violence and death rush to a child's ears far before we think they have reached an "age of understanding." When children hear something they do not understand and realize Mommy and Daddy never talk to them about the issues they are hearing, they may well think it is something bad—something they should not have heard. They feel uncomfortable—even scared. Indeed, they believe they are the one who has done something wrong.

In their literal translation of life, children interpret these feelings to mean there is something "bad" about them for having even heard the issue. Then, instead of taking the issue to their parents, they bury it in fear to avoid any projected repercussions. Whenever children think a question about the issue might upset or anger a parent or other adult, they quickly clam up, burying questions and unpleasant feelings inside, often for a lifetime.

At times, attempting to decipher the underlying meaning of a child's communication may seem more like trying to decipher Egyptian hieroglyphics! We have to really listen, and listen well, to read between the lines. Sometimes communication is not done with words.

Jennifer was twenty-one when she requested assistance to find her birth mother. Although she was of legal age, it was my practice to determine just how prepared a person was for a search, to assure the greatest success in resolving their need to search. I asked Jennifer how her adoptive parents felt about the idea of searching.

Jennifer answered, "My mother says it's just fine with her, but I know it's not."

I asked how she came to the conclusion that her mother did not really support her search.

Jennifer immediately assumed a stiff posture in her chair. With her head turned firmly away from me, her eyes closed tightly, yet cast down toward the floor, she held both hands up in front of her chest, defensively shoving her palms toward me as she mocked, "Go ahead and search, if that's what you want to do. Go ahead."

Returning her hands to her lap, she opened her eyes and looked back at me saying, "That's how she told me it was okay to search. That's how I know she's not happy about it."

In further questioning, I learned that Jennifer's adoptive mother had always taken a similar stance whenever Jennifer broached the subject of her adoption. Ultimately, Jennifer stopped bringing up the subject. Although she suppressed her need to talk about adoption, the questions remained. Not talking about it did not stop her need to know. In fact, it probably intensified her curiosity.

In Jennifer's case, burying her thoughts and feelings caused no irreversible damage. She was a beautiful, talented young lady, preparing to graduate from college. Despite avoiding this very significant topic she had a close relationship with both of her parents, who ultimately supported her search to find a missing piece of her life puzzle. Unfortunately for many, the results may be disastrous.

There are a disproportionate number of adoptees and former foster children in prison. While no one can say with certainty that adoption or foster care is directly related to their criminal behaviors, we hear a hauntingly repeated theme in their stories.

After working for several years in adoption, a turn of events allowed me to open a private practice, which partially involved adoption-specific counseling and consultation. One Friday afternoon an attorney I knew through my work at the adoption agency called. He had been appointed by the court to represent a young man for the attempted murder of his mother. He was certain adoption was the primary factor for his behavior.

"Jerry, you're really stretching for this one! I don't think adoption makes people murder!"

Jerry insisted there was a connection in this case, and urged me to go to the county jail to interview the young man. I said I would think about it, but doubted I would take him up on the offer. However, after a weekend of pondering the request, my curiosity got the better of me. On Monday I called Jerry to make the necessary arrangements for me to go to the jail to meet this adoptee.

A stoic looking young man of eighteen faced me. After telling him why I was there, he said, "No one ever talked to me about my adoption before." After hearing his story, you may be as incensed by that statement as I was.

What Steven knew of his adoption story, he knew only because he was old enough when it began to remember at least bits and pieces of what had happened.

He recalled a woman he presumed to be his birth mother. He remembered a lot of strangers pulling on his body, tearing him out of this woman's arms. He remembered being taken by these strangers to a house, where there were more strangers. He remembered his younger brother being with him.

We began to piece together the puzzle of his adoption.

Although he did not know the reason, it was apparent Steven and his brother were removed from their birth mother and placed in foster care. Steven recalled being moved from house to house, family to family, always with his brother. He thought he might have been about four or five, and his brother was probably a toddler when their journey began.

If his memory is correct, he and his brother were moved approximately fourteen times in less than two years. Then he recalls several "big men wearing all black." These men took Steven and his brother and placed them in a car. He remembers being taken to a big building where there were many children. He said that when they arrived at the building, his brother was "taken away" from him.

As he was living in what we presumed to be a boys' home, he was still able to see his brother each day, usually in the dining hall. One day, his brother was not there. Steven begged repeatedly to see his brother and finally was told, "He's gone. He was adopted." Steven added, "That's when I made the decision never to smile again." He was seven.

Soon thereafter, a couple adopted Steven. He remembered only that they appeared and took him on a long trip. However, the story is much more complex.

I want to make it clear that Steven's adoptive parents are not to blame for his behaviors. From what I can gather, they clearly did everything they knew to make the adoption work. Everything they knew was simply not enough.

Steven, who referred to himself as Native American, believed he was of mixed ancestry. He was unclear about the nationality of his birth father. He was adopted by an Italian-American family that took him on a journey through three states to live in San Antonio with its obviously heavy Hispanic population. Those dynamics alone were so significant. Red flags should have signaled "trouble" even before the adoption, yet were apparently never explored with the adoptive family, and certainly not with Steven.

While we have no knowledge of their reason for choosing to adopt, we know that the family already had one older son, possibly born to them, who Steven referred to as "their golden child." Steven either presumed or overheard that he was adopted as a "playmate" for this older son.

The only two positive memories of his adoption that I recall Steven relating, were that he played baseball and thought he did well at it, and that he loved the family dog. For the most part, he recalled never living up to his parents' expectations and being repeatedly compared to his older, "golden child" brother.

When Steven entered his teens, he began drinking heavily. By the time I met him at age eighteen, he was a severe alcoholic. Whether he overheard something or unconditionally accepted stereotyping of Native Americans, Steven told me, "You know, she (his birth mother) was an alcoholic like Indians are, and that's why they took us from her." I don't believe he actually knew that as a fact, because no one ever discussed his original family with him. However, what is notable is that Steven involved himself in a behavior he believed to be "like" his birth mother. It is quite possible his initial involvement with alcohol was a subconscious effort to gain a sense of "belonging"—in essence, an effort to achieve an attachment to his roots; nevertheless, his own drinking led to other misbehaviors. His family took him to therapists and he was placed in residential psychiatric settings more than once. Steven had also spent previous time in juvenile detention and adult prison.

He had recently been released from prison and returned home when he began drinking heavily. One night he asked his mother for the car keys and when she refused to give them to him, he grabbed a rifle and began chasing his mother. She threw the keys at him and ran from the house. Steven chased her with the rifle, firing shots, which missed her, but landed in the front door of the neighbor's house, where his mother had run for help. He took the keys, raced down the highway in the car, and was quickly stopped by the police.

It seemed curious to me that with all of the mental health treatment, psychiatric placements, prison experiences and the adoption experience itself, no one considered adoption an issue to talk about with Steven. I asked him about this. His response was, "They probably didn't know."

Obviously, that was not true. His family knew. The agency that placed him with the family knew. His parents probably mentioned it to the mental health professionals. Most likely, the police, youth detention and prison authorities knew. Yet no one broached the adoption issue with Steven. Why?

There are only two reasons I can fathom why adoption would not be the primary topic of conversation in every step of the life of a child like Steven.

1) We don't want to talk about issues that are uncomfortable for us, so we don't even hear them.
2) We are totally oblivious to what constitutes a real problem, so, not knowing it's a problem, we don't talk about it.

I say this not to be sarcastic, but to emphasize the critical importance of listening for the real issues, and then making yourself comfortable with those issues that are uncomfortable for you. It is only then that you can help your children resolve their own issues.

Any issue out of the norm is uncomfortable. If something doesn't fit the norm (our norm), there are these uneasy feelings that often push us in the opposite direction. Whether the issue is adoption, abuse, divorce, disability, death, finances, incarceration, sexuality, race, religion, aging, domestic violence, substance abuse, etc., if we aren't comfortable with it, we avoid talking about it.

Recall when someone you know has died. Whether the death was expected or a terribly tragic, untimely occurrence, how often have you thought, or actually said (or, heard others say), "I just don't know what to say to the family"? Our discomfort with the issue probably does not have as much to do with actual physical death, as it does with the emotions surrounding the death.

When we hit a discomfort zone and "don't know what to say," we do one of two things.

1) We say nothing, to avoid the issue.
2) We say everything, to avoid the issue.

The result is, we make everyone as uncomfortable as we are, and the individual needing encouragement is left to suppress thoughts and feelings, which so desperately need to be safely released. Either way, by avoiding the issue, we do a serious injustice to the person and to our relationship with that person.

Facing Roaring Lions

Which of you by taking thought can add one cubit unto his stature?   *— Matthew 6:27*

The following is what I remember being told as an African folk tale. It is a strong statement about what happens when we hit our discomfort zone.

In the jungle where lions roam freely, the young cubs play as their parents spend their days hunting for food.

The oldest of the lions, with his matted hair and toothless snarl, sits alone, hidden in the bush, too old, tired and feeble to hunt any longer. When a herd of antelope comes near, it is the old lion's job to roar ferociously, announcing their arrival.

In terror, the agile antelope race away from the ferocious roar, right into the mouths of the waiting healthy young lions and they are devoured.

The feeble old lion can do nothing but roar. Had the antelope run to the roar they would have been safe.

Most discomforts and fears that send us racing directly into the mouths of healthy lions, waiting to devour us, are related to "losses"—especially losses that make us believe we are without control over a particular situation. Such losses stir up thoughts and feelings of "inadequacy." Thoughts and feelings of inadequacy become roaring lions for most people, and they find themselves running in the wrong direction—away from the roar.

As mirrors reflecting to our children the protocol for dealing with difficult situations, if our manner of facing our own roaring lions is to flee, we reflect to our children that they too, must run from their problems. Likewise, if our manner of facing our own roaring lions is to flee, it also directly influences our ability to discuss roaring lions with others—even our children. Children sense their parents' fears and discomforts. You may only send unspoken clues, however what is not said speaks so much louder than your words.

The sensitivity of children is exceedingly keen. Children, especially very young children, or those who have not been encouraged to express their innermost feelings, do not have sufficient vocabulary or experience to express what they feel. Therefore, their instincts and intuition serve to compensate for this insufficiency. Unfortunately, while they may feel a wide range of emotions, they do not have the means to adequately and appropriately express what they feel. As adult role models, it is our responsibility to help them find the words and become articulate at expressing their feelings. To fulfill this responsibility, we must assure that we are fully comfortable in expressing our own feelings.

The average adult has great difficulty expressing feelings. Many are virtually incapable of expressing their feelings. Most often, when asked what they feel about a given situation, they will respond with a thought—not a feeling. For example, we might ask an adult how they feel about the death of a loved one or the loss of a job or diagnosis of a catastrophic illness. They will likely respond with something like: "I'm just going to have to learn to live with it" or "We'll just have to move ahead." These are thoughts, not feelings. However, we are most happy to agree with their thought and move forward too, avoiding their uncomfortable feelings right along with them.

Over time we learn to trust our feelings (our instincts and intuition) less and less, and we certainly learn not to express our feelings publicly, as we are told, "That's childish;" "You shouldn't think that way;" "You shouldn't feel that way;" "That's foolish;" "Big boys/girls don't cry;" "Just keep a stiff upper lip!" even "You're crazy to feel that way!" we relinquish the gift of trust in our feelings. Instead, we start to apply intellectual interpretation to our emotional experiences. To avoid the disapproval of others, we condition ourselves to suppress feelings that greatly need to be explored, but are no longer socially acceptable for us to hang out in public! Those suppressed feelings become our roaring lions.

When we slam a door in the face of a roaring lion the roaring only increases, becoming more and more frightening. It takes a tremendous amount of energy to keep the door latched when a raging lion is repeatedly smashing against it. As the roaring grows louder and more ferocious, it becomes increasingly difficult to overcome the fear of opening that door.

To assure that doors of communication are not slammed shut on roaring lions, it is essential to be fully alert to the roaring lions you avoid. Face them. Work to resolve them. The relief will be well worth the terror of looking them in the face. Only then, will you be able to help your children face their own roaring lions. You will know you have overcome your own roaring lions, when you can easily talk openly and honestly about former discomfort zone issues with anyone, especially your own children.

The following is a list of many common uncomfortable issues and possible related fears, to alert you to lions that may be roaring for your attention. To quiet roaring lions, you must be fully honest with yourself as you read through this list. If you perceive the least twinge of discomfort with any issue, or recall other issues that cause you discomfort, you are urged to begin resolving your fears about that subject. Seek professional assistance if the roaring persists for several months or longer. Remember, the longer the roaring persists, the longer it will take to tame it. Until the discomfort is resolved for you, your children's lions will continue roaring—louder and louder.

While the problem may be roaring loudly and all those around you may recognize the roar, **you** must be the one to identify and admit there is a problem. Without your own acknowledgment and your own courage to face the roar, there will be no resolution. Unchecked, the roar will only grow louder, as the problem grows bigger.

Identifying Roaring Lions

Check the issue(s) roaring most loudly for you, and check each fear you experience about your roaring lions.

√	Roaring Issues	√	Roaring Fears
	Abuse		Loss of acceptance
	Addiction		Loss of affection
	Adoption		Loss of approval
	Aging		Loss of attention
	Body Image	√	Loss of control *
	Death		Loss of dreams
	Disability		Loss of emotional security
	Divorce		Loss of financial security
	Domestic Violence		Loss of freedom
	Education/Intellect		Loss of independence
	Emotionality of Others		Loss of interaction with others
	Finances		Loss of physical security
	Illness	√	Loss of power *
	Incarceration		Loss of respect of others
	Legal		Loss of self-respect
	Mental Illness		Loss of status
	National Security		Other loss:
	Obesity		
	Personal Security		
	Physical Abuse		
	Physical Appearance		
	Racial Issues		
	Sexual Abuse		
	Sexuality		
	Warfare		
	Other:		

Avoid being too specific in naming your roaring lions. For example, you may specifically fear the repossession of your car. In a literal sense it is the loss of a possession. However, for purposes of identifying your roaring lions, you must determine how that material loss affects you. Does the loss of your car represent your loss of Status, Security, Independence, Respect, etc.?

* √ All Roaring Issues involve a fear of the loss of power and loss of control. These two fears must be recognized and acknowledged for all Roaring Issues, in addition to any other fears related to your Roaring Issues.

Jump-Starting Communication

A good man out of the good treasure of his heart bringeth forth that which is good... for out of the abundance of the heart his mouth speaketh.   — Luke 6:45

Why is it easier to talk about intimate issues with a stranger, than our own child?

I've actually had strangers on elevators (where no one ever talks) tell me the most intimate details of their lives. Between the lobby and fourth floor I've heard domestic violence problems. Between the seventh floor and the ground floor I've heard of infertility problems. Between the garage and the lobby I've heard financial woes. Is it my face? I don't think so. In fact, having a zillion degrees and umpteen years of experience as a therapist, has nothing to do with it.

Mark was one of the first youth I met at the juvenile offenders' facility. He was sixteen, with an athletic build, standing about six foot one or two. He used his size to intimidate other youth, as well as the staff in his dorm. He was both verbally and physically assaultive, always getting himself into trouble. His dorm staff worked hard with him on his behavior problems.

Over the next two years, I only saw Mark occasionally, primarily related to issues with his family. There was a long period of time that I hardly saw him at all, except for his occasional wave as he walked past my office door.

Then one day he came into my office, unannounced. He informed me that he would be leaving in a few days, returning home, and just wanted to say good-bye. I told him I was happy for him and hoped he would do well. I added, "I haven't seen you in a long time, but I'm so pleased you decided to 'clean up your act.' I've heard you were doing well in the program."

Always eager to understand why some people change and others don't, I asked Mark, "I'm really interested in knowing what makes the difference for you guys. Can you tell me what really turned things around for you?"

Without hesitation Mark responded, "Well, you know Miss, it was the time you..."

Now, I'm puffing up, ready to pat myself on the back for my exemplary professional expertise and skills. My goodness, I'd hardly seen him at all, yet I had made the difference!

Mark continued, "...it was the time you asked me, 'What do you get out of it?' that really made the difference for me."

*That was it? "**What do you get out of it?**" That didn't take any professional expertise!*

Pulling myself together to maintain an appearance of professional composure, I asked, "And, what about that made the difference?"

*"You know, it really made me think—what **did** I get out of it? I decided I got nothing out of it, so I decided to stop acting like a fool. I really like myself better this way! Thanks Miss."*

"Oh!" I said. "Well, I'm so pleased for you. You made good choices for yourself." I wished him well and said good-bye, then thought for a long time about my reaction.

It was at that moment I realized "helping" has little to do with diplomas or length of experience. Anyone can say, "What do you get out of it?"

Helping, truly helping; is about caring enough to seize the opportunity to say exactly what is on your heart, with as much love and concern as you have to offer. I could have sat there week after week listening to Mark's bad behavior problems. I could have espoused lines from literature I'd read on the subject. I could have pointed out to him the psychodynamics behind his repeated behavior problems. I could have preached about the merits of good behavior. But, I didn't do any of that. I only cared enough about him to say exactly what had been on my heart at the moment. Anyone can do that! You don't need a degree to say what is on your heart.

To help—to really make a difference, you need to have a genuinely helpful motivation when you say what is on your heart. If your motivation is genuinely caring, results of the intervention will almost always be positive. Remember, you generally get what you expect. People, especially children, sense when you are doing things because you really care about them, or because you want to get things over with in a hurry, look good to others—or possibly even want to hurt them. Again, those unspoken messages are the loudest part of any conversation. It's not **what** you say, but **how** you say it.

At times it will take some soul-searching to check out your motivation for saying what is on your heart, especially if you are in an angry encounter with your child. (Lamentations 3:40 instructs, "Let us search and try our ways, and turn again to the Lord.") Stopping yourself long enough to determine exactly *why* you are going to say whatever it is you feel you need to say, can make all the difference in your relationship with your child. Having a true motivation to help will jump-start your communication efforts.

Even when your motivation is totally loving, there may be times you just don't have the emotional or physical energy, or have become so frustrated or frightened yourself, that you really don't know how to address a difficult situation with your child. At times like that, it is important to step out of the equation and let others who do have the energy and a fresh perspective take over. Turning to an outsider (counselor; member of the clergy; educator; mentor) is not an indication that you do not care about your children. In fact, your willingness to seek such a resource is evidence that you really care about resolving issues with and for your children.

It is just a simple fact: we cannot be all things to all people all of the time—even to our own child. We can however, let go of the steering wheel just long enough to let another person take a fresh, objective look and perhaps nudge the steering wheel just sufficiently to change the course of things. In Mark's case, his family had no choice in turning over the steering wheel. He did something that brought him to a maximum-security institution—taking the steering wheel totally out of their hands. I am grateful to have been at the right place at the right time, to nudge the wheels ever so slightly to make a difference in his life. I suppose that just goes to say that sometimes it takes a "mechanic" to jump-start communication with your child, for you.

Keep Communication Flowing

...he which hath begun a good work in you will perform it
until the day of Jesus Christ. — *Philippians 1:6*

Returning to unsolicited disclosures from strangers on elevators—there are some very good reasons that happens.

Not that I am proud of it, but it is true, I became a social worker before I became a Christian. Then, that day I reached into the drawer of a hospital bed stand and began reading the Bible—was I surprised! The principles I had been taught in secular training for social work were right there in the Bible! It was reassuring to know that!

In the next several chapters, there are five of those principles I would like to share with you. These are basic principles professional counselors use to jump-start and maintain a flow of communication with their clients. While using these principles professionally, then beginning to change within myself, I found them to be very helpful in maintaining open communication with my own children. I believe it is time that these principles be placed in the hands of those who need them most, and pray that they be used with the greatest sensitivity, to enhance relationships between parents and their children.

Principle I: Establish Trust

A talebearer revealeth secrets: but he that is of a faithful
spirit concealeth the matter. — *Proverbs 11:13*

Why would a stranger trust you enough to share confidences with you? They don't even know you!

What they do know is that you won't hurt them. You are unlikely to hurt them physically, and more importantly, you won't hurt them emotionally. You probably will never see them again. Therefore, you won't have opportunities to blind-side them with their misdeeds, by throwing them back in their face one day when they least expect it. You won't have any opportunity to belittle or tease them about the transgressions they shared with you, when they foul up once again. Since you don't know them, odds are you won't embarrass them or shatter their life by telling their deepest secret to their boss, neighbor, friend or especially another family member. In fact, as a stranger, your kindly nods provide just the feeling of acceptance and comfort they were seeking. There is very little risk involved in sharing confidences with a stranger.

On the other hand, there is great risk involved in sharing confidences with someone you live with twenty-four hours a day, every day of the year. There is ample time and opportunity to blind-side, belittle, tease and embarrass a family member, especially the most vulnerable family member—your child.

Method 1: Maintain A High Level Of Sensitivity
Blessed be God... God of all comfort: Who comforteth us in all our tribulation, that we may be able to comfort them which are in any trouble, by the comfort wherewith we ourselves are comforted of God. — II Corinthians 1:3-4

A. Accept a Person Right Where He Is
Trust is fundamental to any relationship. The first step in establishing trust is acceptance. Accepting a person exactly where they are, whether you agree with them or not, is critical to gaining their trust. For example, if they are angry, you must genuinely accept the fact that they are angry and acknowledge their anger. If they are in pain, you must sincerely accept the fact that they are feeling pain and acknowledge that pain. If they are in grieving, you must accept the fact that they are grieving and acknowledge their grief. That does not mean you will indefinitely continue to help perpetuate any harmful or inappropriate beliefs or behaviors that may accompany their

current state. It means you will never tell a crying child to "Buck up, buddy! Big boys and girls don't cry!" Or ever tell a heartbroken teenager, "Hey! You've got no idea what grief is, so cheer up!" It means you never tell anyone that they don't feel whatever they've expressed feeling! It simply means you are sensitive enough to accept and acknowledge the feelings and beliefs they express as fact, right from the beginning, and listen to their reality—not impose yours.

B. Never Exploit or Abuse a Known Weakness

Sensitivity is also required to maintain trust, once you gain it. When you misuse any information you have gained from your relationship with your child, it breaks his trust in you. While a baby may unconditionally trust its parent, as the child grows and experiences teasing or embarrassment or ridicule, especially at the hands of his parent, trust deteriorates and erodes, significantly. While the teasing may seem insignificant, even loving to you, it may not be received as insignificant and loving by your child. As a parent, you must develop the sensitivity to know when to hold 'em and know when to fold 'em. Never use what you know about a child to tease him, unless and until you are completely certain he comfortably accepts it as a joke.

In my own memory bank I recall safe, playful, even loving horseplay with my father evolving into incessant, painful tickling sessions. Why he could not stop himself from tickling me until my mother literally had to scream at him to stop is beyond my comprehension, even to this day. He was a loving father in all other ways. However, this teasing, as he viewed it, went on until I ultimately learned to stay away from him, physically. I learned one more trick to avoid the teasing—I stopped being ticklish. In essence, I stopped feeling.

In my counseling work, I have met other women who have had similar experiences with their fathers and interpreted it as abuse—one woman in particular actually interpreted this behavior as sexual abuse. While I fortunately never interpreted my own father's behavior that way, his apparent inability to acquire the sensitivity to know when to stop the teasing was detrimental to me, and most unfortunately in some ways, detrimental to our relationship.

When I had my own children, I remembered those tickling experiences. While I tickled my children, I knew one tickle was enough. As the children became aware of what was coming when they saw my "tickle-finger" spring forth, I went one step further—I began tickling by "remote control"! They laughed just as hard when they saw my tickle-finger momentarily wiggling closer and closer but never touching, as they had when I actually tickled them. Even as adults, now I sometimes tease them with my tickle-finger, and it still evokes a giggle. It may seem a small thing to those who aren't bothered by tickling, but I am grateful to have been given the sensitivity to be able to look at my own painful experiences with it, and not inflict them upon my children. I am grateful to have developed the sensitivity required not to break my children's trust in me.

Trust is essential to your relationship with your child. To maintain that trust, you must develop the sensitivity to refrain from ever using anything you know about your child, especially anything he may be easily upset by, in a manner that would hurt your relationship with him, even the fact that he's ticklish. Develop the sensitivity to know what hurts your child, especially what hurts him way deep down inside, and never use it in a way that will break his trust in you. Instead, know what gives your child joy and lavish it upon him!

Method 2: Assure That You Are Speaking The Same Language.

> *And the whole earth was of one language and of one speech.* — Genesis 11:1

Often we think we are expressing ourselves very clearly, only to have the person we are talking to, totally misunderstand what we have said. There are a number of reasons we misunderstand our communication with each other. Sometimes we simply have not said exactly what we meant to say, sometimes, one or the other of us is just not listening. At other times we are using expressions or language that simply "does not compute" with the other person. This is especially a possibility when we are speaking across generational lines. One good way to assure that you have conveyed your message clearly, is to ask the person you are speaking to, to repeat the information back to you in their own words.

When you are trying to express really critical information, it is important to refrain from using confusing or unclear jargon, or from joking or using sarcasm. I have been notoriously sarcastic, more so in the past than I am now. However, my awareness of the fact that some people don't get the joke, and interpret exactly what you say—literally—did not come until rather late in life.

While I was interviewing candidates for a job opening at the youth facility, one of the questions I typically ask job applicants, was to express what they see as their own strengths and their own weaknesses. This particular applicant responded to that question by giving a reasonable list of strengths, including his ability to learn quickly, be punctual, etc. Then he stopped. I asked him to now share what he saw as his weaknesses. He said angrily, "Why do you keep asking me if I'm weak? I'm not weak. I never back down when I'm right." Well, for my purposes, I got the answer I needed to make my decision, however, it was clear that his interpretation of the words I was using, was not the same as my intention in using them!

Just the other morning after church, a friend's young son came up to me and whispered, "Your money's sticking out." It took a few seconds to understand what he was talking about, but when I did, I glanced at my purse and noted that indeed, several dollar bills were clearly exposed. I thanked him and as I was stuffing the money back in my purse and zipping up the compartment, I sarcastically commented, "So, how much did you get?" At first, he smiled and said, "None." However, several minutes later he came back over to me and asked, "Why would I tell you about your money showing, if I took some?" Actually, I never thought he took any money, but my off-handed and inappropriate sarcasm certainly did nothing to build trust between this child and myself. Sometimes I slip and revert back to my sarcastic days. Generally, when I do, I regret it.

Method 3: Maintain Confidences

Set a watch, O Lord, before my mouth; keep the door of my lips.   — *Psalm 141:3*

When your child shares a confidence with you, it must remain just that, a confidence. Not because it is the law, those laws don't apply to families and friends, but you do not betray a confidence because in doing so, it will destroy his trust in you. Continued betrayal will ultimately destroy your relationship with your child, altogether.

Unless your child, or any person for that matter, has shared that he may cause harm to himself or others, there is no reason to share his confidence, *without his permission,* except to be malicious. However, you **absolutely must report issues of potential harm to self or others, i.e., child abuse, suicide or murder.** This is so important, that it bears emphasis.

As I am writing we are experiencing the anniversary of one of the most horrible tragedies in our nation's history. The aftermath of the massacre of students at Columbine High School in Littleton, Colorado has indicated that the parents of at least one of the perpetrators knew their child was building bombs in their home. The news media has reported that these parents did not report this knowledge, because their child was already in trouble with the law, and they believed that reporting further criminal activity might result in the incarceration of their son.

I say this not to sit in judgment of those parents, because parents do what they believe is best with the information and strengths and weaknesses available to them at the moment. These parents apparently did what they thought was right. Only through 20/20 hindsight do they now most probably know, their belief was absolutely wrong. May every parent, learn from this tragic 20/20 hindsight.

It is never right to cover up threatening, dangerous or criminal behaviors of our children. While as I write, we have not heard from the parents of the young perpetrators of the Columbine massacre, I would venture to say, they are second-guessing themselves every minute of their lives now. They are likely thinking, "It would have been better to have our child alive and in jail or prison, than dead with the reputation of being a mass murderer." They have to be thinking that, and now there is nothing they can do. There is no hope.

Never allow yourself to be placed in such a helpless, hopeless position. Recall, I said I wanted my 20/20 hindsight to allow other parents to know that "without a doubt there is hope"? I so wish I could have shared this 20/20 hindsight with those parents. I can only imagine their grief. I pray others will learn from their 20/20 hindsight, as well. Always—always report potential harm to self or others. Always! You never want to live what those parents are living. If you fear the law, at least seek help from a member of the clergy, a counselor, an educator, a physician—someone—anyone who may provide an opportunity to stop the behavior before it ends in a hopeless tragedy such as this one.

If, when evil cometh upon us, as the sword, judgment, or pestilence, or famine, we stand before this house, and in thy presence, (for thy name is in this house,) and cry unto thee in our affliction, then thou wilt hear and help.
                                        — *II Chronicles 20:9*

Having said that, it may sound like a contradiction to say, "Always maintain a child's confidences." The principle of always maintaining a child's confidences has one major exception. When there is a possibility of harm to self or others, you must break the confidence—you must.

However, under ordinary circumstances, when a child shares a burden that is on his heart, finally revealing a most vulnerable aspect of his life, he is taking a huge risk. He trusts you sufficiently to take that risk with you. That is an honor, not to be taken lightly. He is indicating he trusts you to use the shared information to strengthen your relationship—to support him, not to harm him with that information. Use what you learn in confidence, only to help.

Sometimes, when we have been entrusted with confidential information, we feel that using that information as an "inside joke" will draw us even closer to the one supplying it. When used to help, that may very well be what happens. However, when used to tease or belittle, calling attention to a perceived flaw will cause a deep rift in the relationship. Why would they ever again take you into their confidence, if you are only going to use that information to make them feel small?

Sharing confidences requires trust between two parties. When that trust is broken, it is virtually impossible to totally erase the resulting scar. The relationship will never be one of full trust again. Never use information you have received in confidence to tease or belittle your child, even in jest. If it is not funny to your child, it will never be funny to your relationship.

Principle II: Remain Objective

...ye shall hear the small as well as the great; ye shall not be afraid of the face of man; for the judgment is God's: and the cause that is too hard for you, bring it unto me, and I will hear it   — *Deuteronomy 1:17*

Why would a total stranger share his darkest secret with you? Because, you are not going to become emotional!

A stranger knows you won't shout angry epithets at them because they have messed up your life. They know you won't cry, because they hurt your feelings. They know you won't run away in shock and horror, because you are disgusted by the behavior they describe to you.

With a stranger, you are not emotionally affected by the problem. Being an objective outsider, you won't be moved to emotion, which often results in espousing caustic remarks, asserting critical opinions or running away—abandonment! They only want to release a burden. They only want a sounding board. They do not want criticism. They certainly don't want to be shamed. They just want someone to listen. Your objectivity makes you a safe listener.

Often, that is all your child wants—a safe ear.

Method 1: Remain Emotionally Separate

...a time to embrace and a time to refrain from embracing.   *— Ecclesiastes 3:5*

This is the most difficult method to employ, especially with your own children, but it is also a method of great importance to your relationship with them. You only have to assess any abruptly terminated conversation, to understand why this is so important. Recall the moment in the conversation when the topic abruptly changed, the conversation cooled or was actually cut short. In all likelihood, the door closed at the moment someone became the least bit emotional.

Most people have great difficulty standing still when someone becomes emotional. Emotionality is a very common roaring lion. The first inclination is to run—avoid it! It is difficult enough to deal with our own emotions. It is even more difficult to deal with the emotions of someone else. We rarely stay around long enough to see the emotional issue through to a successful conclusion.

This is exactly the reason you must resolve your own roaring lions sufficiently, so that the sound of them does not cause you to run. It is the only way you can stand still long enough to effectively deal with other people's roaring lions—including your children's. When you become emotional, you become part of the problem, not a part of the solution to the problem. As difficult as it may be, to effectively help resolve the problem you must stand back—assess the roar and objectively face it without getting emotional!

Method 2: Give Only Non-judgmental Feedback

Judge not, that ye be not judged. For with what judgment ye judge, ye shall be judged: and with what measure ye mete, it shall be measured to you again. — Matthew 7:1

As a novice social worker, I actually believed that to "remain non-judgmental," meant I was not to have values. For a very brief time, I found myself actually telling myself that any behavior a client shared with me was all right! It quickly became very clear to me that this was not what the phrase "remain non-judgmental," meant! I realized that without holding strong values of my own, I certainly could not help others find their own direction. However, that did not mean forcing my values and beliefs on others.

Being non-judgmental simply means, not falling out of your chair when someone tells you something that is totally incompatible with your own values and beliefs. This definitely requires facing your own roaring lions. If you fall off your chair, or even indicate that you might, when someone tells you their deepest secret, it is highly unlikely they will actually tell you any more. If you want your child to be open with you, get a firm grip on your chair! That means, sit still and be quiet until you've heard him out! If you don't, he won't tell you vital information you need to know to ever lead him to where you want him to be.

Working with offenders who had committed the most heinous of crimes, my goal was of course, to help them recognize the error of their ways. I certainly did not support their behaviors. In fact, I was most often appalled, even sickened by their behaviors. However, if my goal was to help them stop those behaviors, it hardly behooved me to scream in horror, throw up my hands with repulsion, become red-faced with rage and run from the room. If I in any way wanted their values to more closely match mine, I had to react in a way that would **lead** them to a new way of thinking.

To help your child, you must withhold your judgment! That is extremely difficult to do as a parent. Here is a child you love dearly, living in your home, making a decision to behave in a manner that goes totally against your values and beliefs. In fact, it is likely a decision that you know will lead to trouble. It is so hard to let that go. The first inclination will probably be to **make** him see it your way.

Don't do it!

As long as he's talking, keep him talking! Unless the behavior is life threatening, you still have an opportunity to build a relationship that will lead your child to safer ground. Preaching, moralizing, demanding, forcing, manipulating, even coercing are communication roadblocks. You want to **lead** your child to make a better decision for himself. To do this, you must be on very solid footing, yourself. Sit still. Do not react, yet. Assess your own roaring lions. Resolve those that are still roaring. Be very clear in your own mind about your own values and form your questions to lead your child to those values. That's right—questions! In times of emotion, statements can be, and most often are, judgmental—generally made as statements of "fact." Therefore, any statement you make is likely to sound accusatory and will shut the door to further communication. Questions are more likely to indicate that you want to know more.

Here is a possible outline for remaining non-judgmental:

1) Make yourself aware of the problem (Proverbs 2: 1-6)
2) Pray (Psalm 138:1-3; Matthew 21:22)
3) Maintain composure (Proverbs 29:11)
4) Ask a leading question (Matthew 7:8; James 1:5)
5) Pray (Psalm 138:1-3; Matthew 21:22)
6) Remain composed at the answer (Proverbs 20:3; Matthew 5:9)
7) Ask another leading question (Proverbs 2:1-6)
8) Pray (Psalm 105:4)
9) Remain composed at the answer (Ecclesiastes 9:10)
10) Ask one more leading question (Proverbs 2:1-6)
11) Pray (Psalm 88:1-2; Matthew 7:7-8)
12) Remain composed, etc. (Proverbs 20:3; Philippians 4:7)

   NOTICE: At no point is there room for preaching, moralizing, criticizing, demanding or judging.

To encourage the communication to keep flowing, avoid these tactics at all costs. First of all, the problem you see on the surface is not the **real** problem at all. What you want and need to do is discover the reason **behind** the behavior. Non-judgmental, leading questions will take you there. When the reasons **behind** the behavior are resolved, it is likely the behavior will resolve itself.

Method 3: Lead, By Using Open-ended Questions

So he fed them according to the integrity of his heart; and guided them by the skillfulness of his hands.

—*Psalm 78:72*

One of the most effective methods for finding the real reasons for your child's behavior is to use open-ended questioning. The strategy is to ask questions that will elicit more information. Your open-ended questions are a means to lead your child to recognize the right answers for himself.

As the parent, we seem to feel we must provide all the answers. My 20/20 parenting hindsight indicates this is erroneous thinking on our part. First of all let's just face it, just because we're older and probably wiser does not mean we have all the answers to all the problems. Secondly, by giving our children all the answers (whether we really have them or not), they never have the opportunity to learn how to solve their own problems. Thirdly, they also begin to resent our all-knowing attitude and stop listening to us.

Very young children can find their own good answers to their problems, especially when they are carefully led to find them. Even we, as adults, do not like being told what to do. Answers have so much more impact and meaning when we realize them for ourselves.

EXAMPLES OF OPEN-ENDED QUESTIONS

Open-ended questions encourage a dialogue about issues of concern. Closed-ended questions diminish any potential dialogue. Each results in exactly what it says it does: open-ended questions OPEN conversation; closed-ended questions CLOSE the conversation.

Open Ended Question	Possible Response	Closed-ended Question	Possible Response
What happened at the store today?	Some description of what occurred.	Did you steal something from the store?	Yes/No/Silence
Who was with you when it happened?	List of persons involved or admission of solo activity.	Was that thug, Bobby with you?	Yes/No/Silence

Open Ended Question	Possible Response	Closed-ended Question	Possible Response
How did you make the decision to take the CD?	Some type of explanation of the process involved in the offense.	It was your idea, wasn't it?	Yes/No/Silence
What did you think would happen when you took it?	Some explanation, probably of how they thought they'd get away with it.	Didn't you realize you'd get caught?	Yes/No/Silence
What generally happens when people get caught stealing?	Some explanation of known previous consequences.	Don't you know you can go to jail for that?	Yes/No/Silence
What do you think about those consequences?	Some statement about the consequences that might happen.	Do you want to go to jail?	Yes/No/Silence
What do you think is the best way to resolve this, now that it's happened?	Dialogue about possible consequences.	You know you're going to get what you deserve, don't you?	Yes/No/Silence
How are you feeling about what you did?	Some explanation of current feelings.	I've never been so disgusted with you in my life.	Silence

It is difficult to know exactly what the actual answers might be in a real situation. However, by reviewing the questions and trying to answer them yourself, you will note that open-ended questions require some dialogue. They generally cannot be answered with a monosyllable. The goal of the open-ended question is to keep the conversation going in order to learn as much as possible from the exchange.

Changing Hearts

A new heart also will I give you, and a new spirit will I put within you; and I will take away the stony heart out of your flesh and I will give you a heart of flesh. And I will put my spirit within you, and cause you to walk in my statutes... — *Ezekiel 36:26-27*

Locking a lion in a cage can control its behavior. Confined to a small, secured area the animal can but roar or whimper, causing no real harm. But what happens when the cage is opened?

We can control our children's behavior in the same way. By confining them to their room, not allowing them to leave the house or yard, their behavior is similarly controlled. Once the restriction is over, will the behavior be changed?

Principle III: Get Past The Behavior

...for the Lord seeth not as man seeth; for man looketh on the outward appearance, but the Lord looketh on the heart. — *I Samuel 16:7*

The behavior is not the real problem. Sure, it is annoying, possibly even dangerous; however it is not the real problem you are facing with your child. The behavior is only a symptom of your child's underlying beliefs, which trigger the behavior. Those *beliefs* are the real problem. Your child believes there is good reason for the behavior, or he would behave differently. If you want to change the behavior, it is necessary

to change the beliefs causing that behavior. To assuredly change un-
desired behavior, the very **heart** of the child must change.

Method: Probing

Ask, and it shall be given you; seek, and ye shall find;
knock, and it shall be opened unto you. — *Matthew 7:7*

To change the heart of your child, you must lead him to believe,
for himself, that his thoughts and feelings about his behavior need
to change. It is your method of leading, not pushing or pulling that
will expose the real reason for his belief that the behavior is necessary.
To do that, you must learn as much as possible about your child. He
probably has no idea that his own beliefs are triggering his unproductive behaviors. Pray. Be patient. It will take time. Explore with
him to find the reasons behind the behavior.

EXAMPLE: PROBING, BY USING OPEN-ENDED QUESTIONS TO LEAD
A CHILD TO A CHANGE OF HEART.
Problem: Child has stolen a CD from a store.

Parent:	You have a CD that doesn't belong to you. We need to decide what we are going to do about this. Tell me what it was that caused you to take it?
Child:	I wanted it.
Parent:	What was the reason you wanted it?
Child:	I liked it.
Parent.	What was it you especially liked about that particular CD?
Child:	I dunno.
Parent:	Well, you said you liked it. Tell me what it was you liked about it.
Child:	Nothin'.
Parent:	If you really didn't like it, why did you want it?
Child:	I was going to give it away.
Parent:	Who were you going to give it to?
Child:	This guy.
Parent:	Which guy is that?
Child:	This guy at school.

Parent: What was the reason you wanted to give it to
          him?
Child: He asked me to get it for him.
Parent: What made you want to get it for him?
Child: I had to.
Parent: Oh. I thought you wanted to get it for him. Now I
          hear you saying that you felt you had to get it for
          him. I'm wondering what it was that made you feel
          you had to get it for him?

We're getting to something that appears to be well beyond stealing. The behavior—stealing—is not the real problem. No matter how
well and how often you have taught your child not to steal, he may
find himself in a situation where his own beliefs override anything
you've taught him. The belief behind the behavior is the problem! If,
as in the example above, something else is going on, hang in there.
Pray. Your probing is working! Stay calm, remain patient, refrain
from becoming judgmental, and keep probing and exploring with
open-ended questions. You will find the real problem, your child's
belief that the behavior was necessary, and then have opportunities
to help him resolve it.

By comparison, what if the parent had done this?

EXAMPLE: DEMANDING, BY PUSHING AND PULLING FOR AN-
SWERS.

   Problem: Child has stolen a CD from the store, but has a
            different parent!
Parent: I know you stole a CD from the store. Why did you
          do that? Why didn't you just ask for the money?
          What is wrong with you?
Child: I dunno.
Parent: You know not to steal.
Child: Uh-huh.
Parent: So why would you steal? Haven't we taught you
          better? Don't you know better? Do you realize
          what could happen? This is embarrassing.
Child: (silence)
Parent: I don't know what to do with you any more.

Child:	(silence)
Parent:	Don't just sit there. Tell me what you are going to do about this.
Child:	(silence)
Parent:	Tell me now. What are you going to do?
Child:	I dunno.
Parent:	Well figure it out. You got yourself into this mess, now how are you going to get yourself out?
Child:	(silence)
Parent:	Well?
Child:	(silence)

The difference between leading by "probing," versus pushing and pulling by "demanding," is that in leading you set yourself up from the beginning as an ally. You say, "What are *we* going to do about this?" Or, you might say, "Let's talk about this." You are indicating at the outset that you are there because you care about him and want to help, not just because you're mad and want to punish him. Then, when you form leading open-ended questions, you indicate that you are interested in answers, because they require more than a "yes/no/ don't know" response or no response at all. Notice that pushing and pulling does not leave much room for response, while open-ended questioning virtually requires a relatively meaningful response. By remaining consistent in using open-ended questions, you will elicit additional information that will help you reach beyond the observable behavior, to discover the hidden reasons for the problem.

Also, notice that by probing you allow your child an opportunity to develop his trust in you. You are not immediately backing him into a losing corner by forcing him to answer immediately with the only option you give him—yours!

As you probe, it becomes clear that your efforts are to assure a win/win outcome. Your child may answer tentatively at first, as he subtly explores your position. He is actually observing your reactions at the same time you are exploring for reasons behind the behavior. As you probe, your child is assessing what he can safely reveal to you. Will you become judgmental or angry? Will you reject him? What type of punishment will result—especially if he tells you the whole truth and nothing but the truth?

Discipline is not important at this stage of the problem. To assure the consequences of any discipline are effective, if and when punishment is administered, the punishment must mean something to your child. If you punish the *behavior* you are missing an important opportunity to teach your child the proverbial lesson you are trying to teach. This is why it is critical to understand the *belief* your child has about the need for his behavior. The most effective discipline will address his *belief*—more than his behavior. Keep probing! As you withhold judgment and avoid confrontation by continuing to probe calmly with open-ended questions, your child feels safer and safer about revealing more and more about his beliefs. Respect what he is sharing. Use what he shares with you to know your child better. Remember; never use what he shares with you against him! Never use it to belittle him or to get the upper hand, and never use what you learn in a manner that breaks his trust in you.

Following are several suggestions to keep communication flowing with children. At first, using them may feel awkward, perhaps even artificial, but keep going! Any change feels awkward and uncomfortable at first, and change takes time. Leading a child to solid ground requires some discomfort and time—a great deal of time. However, when you begin noticing the doors it opens for you, it will become second nature.

Warning! Once I began leading my own children through open doors of communication, I realized I'd created a monster. Now, I had to face more and more of my own roaring lions, to help them face theirs. They were telling me things I really didn't want to know! Well, actually I did want to know, I needed to know, I just wasn't ready to deal with them all. The work had just begun. I had to prepare and stay prepared!

COMMUNICATION DOOR SLAMMERS & DOOR OPENERS

On the left are examples of statements that slam doors on communication.

On the right are examples of statements that potentially open doors of communication.

Communication Door Slammers (Close Ended Comments Or Questions)	Communication Door Openers (Open Ended Comments Or Questions)
"That's ridiculous." "You're crazy." "How dumb can you be?" "How can you even say something like that?"	"That's a new idea for me. Tell me more about it." "I'm not sure I follow you. Could you explain further?"
"I don't have time for that now." "Can't you see I'm busy" "Don't interrupt me. I'm doing something important here!"	"That's interesting. Can we discuss it as soon as I finish this project?" "Maybe you could give me a hand, and we can talk while we finish this project."
"I don't need to hear that from you." "I don't want to hear that out of your mouth!"	"I'm really sorry to hear you say that. Can you help me understand what makes you think that?"
"Get Real!" "Duh!" "Wise-mouth!" "Brilliant!" & other sarcastic comments.	"That's really something to think about! Tell me how you came to that conclusion."
"That's your problem, not mine." "You got yourself into this mess, now get yourself out!" "Don't ask me!"	"That's a big problem. What are your thoughts about resolving it?" "That's a big problem. What can I do to help you work it out?"
"You're doing that all wrong." "I can't believe you don't know how to do that!" "Any moron could figure that out!"	"I may know an easier way to do that. May I show you?" "Looks like you could use some help. May I?"
"No. We're not getting that. It costs too much."	"Sorry. It's not in the budget today. What do you think we could do to start saving for it?"
"You don't know what you're talking about."	"Let's see what we can find out about that. I wonder where we could find that information?"
"You know better than to do that." "How could you do that?" "What were you thinking?"	"I'm not sure I explained that very well, before. Let's talk about that some more." "Tell me what you understood about that."

Communication Door Slammers (Close Ended Comments Or Questions)	Communication Door Openers (Open Ended Comments Or Questions)
"Now you've done it." "Give it to me. I'll do it."	"Let's figure out how we can fix that." "Can I help you with that?"
"Maybe." "I don't think so."	"I'm just not sure right now. Let's talk about that some more after dinner."
"No."	"Can we talk about how I feel about that?"
"Just do it, already."	"Can I help you get started on that?"
"You think you're so smart."	"That's one idea. Can we talk about others?"

Comforting Discipline

*Chasten thy son while there is hope, and let not thy soul
spare for his crying.* — *Proverbs 19:18*

O kay! Let's talk about discipline. It is not my favorite topic! In
fact, you most likely think that I'm pretty lenient, with all
the stories of ignoring misbehavior and not even seeming
to notice when I've been disrespected.

Truthfully, I am very frugal in dispensing discipline. In fact, I
rarely find formal discipline necessary. This of course was not true
when I was raising my own children. Then I dispensed discipline frequently—very frequently. There were the usual swats on the hands
and behinds; confinements to rooms; toy restrictions; TV restrictions; grounding restrictions; driving restrictions; restrictions upon
restrictions, generally accompanied by loud, caustic remarks. Now,
with some 20/20 hindsight, I recognize that the frequency of the restrictions alone was clear evidence that they were *not* effective. If they
were so effective, why did I have to repeat them, time and time again?
In fact, had I ever reflected on the frequency of my own punishment
as a child, I would have noted that all those spankings and confinements to my room never changed my own behavior one iota.

With a great deal of self-examination on the matter of discipline,
I realized that children, especially those beyond two years of age, are
fully capable of verbally exploring their own choices of behavior and
actually quite capable of setting their own, usually effective, consequences with the help of some productive leading and probing.

Punishment for the sake of punishment is rarely effective, however, there are those times it cannot be avoided.

*Not long ago, I was in a classroom with a large number of trou-
bled teens, when suddenly, without forewarning I observed a very pe-
tite, feminine girl viciously expectorate toward a nearby student. The
hideous substance landed on the pant-leg of the boy sitting across the
aisle. I was astonished. Even I have my limits, and spitting is way up
there at the top of my "do not" list.*

*The facility had rigid guidelines for discipline and although I rarely
used them, I knew what to do. Without hesitation, I enforced them.
Veronica was sent to the equivalent of detention hall and a written
report was made. She was gone from the classroom for the remainder
of the day.*

*In the meantime, the ten most exemplary students had been se-
lected to participate in an outing for a special community project. Being selected was an honor bestowed only on the best-behaved students.
The morning following the spitting episode, I noticed Veronica prancing
around campus in one of the brightly colored T-shirts that had been
distributed to those ten youth so honorably selected to participate in
the special off-campus outing. I inquired as to why she was wearing
the special shirt and was summarily informed that she was participating in the special community event. Needless to say, I was a major
step beyond displeased.*

First, we don't reward people for misbehaving. I think that is in
the category of simple logic.

Second, because in my mind the physical aspects of the behavior
required immediate intervention and Veronica was removed from
the "scene of the crime" to avoid further escalation to possible physical danger, no one had any idea why the behavior occurred. No one
had talked to Veronica about her behavior, and certainly not about
her reasoning behind the behavior. She had immediately been sent
to a detention room where she was expected to complete her school-
work—that's all. Now she was going to be out prancing around town,
being rewarded for her misbehavior.

Third, what could she possibly have learned from those two days
of her life that would stop her from spitting to resolve her problems
in the future? Because no one ever explored her behavior, let alone
beyond her behavior, to learn about her belief that she needed to spit
on someone, she received no effective consequences. In fact, removing her from the classroom only resolved **my** problem, not hers. How

unhappy do you think she was at being removed from a classroom? Most kids delight in spending a day out of classes. I doubt she was in any discomfort that would have made her think about her actions.

Fourth, when more than one person is charged with "parenting" a child it is beneficial if all involved at least **appear** to be in agreement. Now we had a situation of "good cop/bad cop" and while I find it necessary to occasionally assume the role of "bad cop" and do so with no hesitation, another's failure to support the discipline had set up a situation of "divide and conquer."

Essentially, Veronica had gotten everything she wanted. She apparently had a beef with the young man she spat on, although no one knows what the problem was, and she was removed from having to deal with him. All of the youth relished the possibility of getting off campus for a thirty minute doctor visit, let alone for a whole day of fun and games, so by dividing and conquering she was actually rewarded with that coveted experience, thanks to an unsupportive "parenting partner."

Fifth, is that once we reward someone for misbehavior and compound that with the failure to be in one accord in enforcing consequences, it is virtually impossible to undo the resulting damage. In fact, rewarding the misbehavior served to validate it, only reinforcing Veronica's belief that she was justified in spitting on the boy and more so, could probably repeat the behavior with little or no consequences in the future. There was no learning gained from the experience, except perhaps mine. I was once again reinforced in the belief that discipline is rarely effective.

In reviewing the files of most juvenile offenders I've worked with, their first offense was never robbery or murder. I think we all know what their first offense was, because most of us did it! Taking candy from the grocery store is generally the first crime most of these youth had successfully accomplished. The difference between them and most of us is that they either did not get caught, or when they were caught, they were either beaten for the behavior or nothing at all was done about it. Occasionally, the behavior was even rewarded. Avoiding consequences for the first offense led to pushing the boundaries just a bit further—and just a bit further after that, and a little further after that, ad infinitum. For example, while the spitting incident was not Veronica's first offense, it would undoubtedly now, not be her last. She had just pushed the boundaries even a little further, and by dividing and conquering, she was actually rewarded for her behavior.

Failure to be in one accord is a critical issue in multi-parent households. It is not unusual for the caretakers of children to disagree on discipline issues; however a conflict in styles of discipline is flatly ineffective.

What if the co-owners of a business totally disagree on procedures?

Ben is demanding the company's esteemed Cherry Buyer only purchase Oregon Bing cherries for the Cherry Fluff Ice Cream recipe. Jerry insists on Maraschino cherries shipped in from China. Back and forth they argue, as Ben tells their highly respected Cherry Buyer, "Oregon" and Jerry demands, "China"! "Oregon!" "China!" "Oregon!" "China!" The result? Possibly no Cherry Fluff Ice Cream at all, and certainly a very confused Cherry Buyer who, although valued by the company, may ultimately throw up his hands in dismay and walk out. Or, perhaps he will take the bull by the horns and, regardless of what Ben & Jerry want, order the rare Surinam cherry, which is actually not a cherry at all. Quite a costly consequence in any case! They lose credibility with their valued Cherry Buyer, they lose money on the purchase of the wrong cherries or they lose sales of their prized Cherry Fluff Ice Cream. The bottom line is that when co-CEOs do not resolve their differences, everyone loses!

The same holds true for co-CEOs in the Parenting Business. Is the child to follow the instructions of Parent Permissive, or defer to the commands of Parent Inflexible? Not only is the child confused, but without agreement between the co-leaders, as the child matures, he will make his own decisions, which may be in total opposition to either leader.

To effectively serve as joint family CEOs, points of disagreement, especially on discipline styles, must be resolved. This is a leadership problem and will require significant communication between the co-CEO's to ever resolve it. When the leaders do not resolve the conflict, the child may find his own resources to deal with the resulting confusion. The results can be deadly.

Javier's father had spent over twenty years in military service by the time I met him. He was rigid in his discipline of all five of his children, expecting them to respond like soldiers to his each and every command.

He was unbending in meting out rather brutal punishment if they did not comply. As he was often away from the home on military assignment, Javier's mother most often gave in to her children's every wish, to compensate for the absence of their father and especially to counteract his harsh discipline while he was at home.

Javier was a relatively quiet sixteen year old, rarely voicing his desires, but deeply hoping that the few times he did ask for something his wish might be acknowledged, if not fulfilled. During one of his father's extended absences from home, Javier asked his mother if he could begin taking Driver's Ed classes. She assessed that her son was doing relatively well in school and rarely gave her any problems. He rarely asked for any special privileges, so, she signed the necessary papers and Javier happily began learning to drive. He knew he would probably never have his own car until he could buy it himself, more due to financial reasons than the rigidity of his father, but he was pleased that, like many of his friends, he would ultimately be able to drive a car, legally.

Several weeks after Javier began Drivers Ed classes, he raced home from school to inform his mother that the class would begin actual hands-on driving the next day. He was elated. Bursting through the front door he started to yell for his mother, when he ran directly into his father who had returned home earlier than expected from his military assignment and intentionally planted himself just inside the front door. Javier's excitement immediately turned to horror. He had never been given a reason, but he knew his father opposed his learning to drive.

Although his mother uttered some words of resistance, his father made Javier remove his clothes and beat him about his body with a leather strap. The next day Javier's father drove him to the school and made him stand silently, while he demanded that Javier be withdrawn from the Driver's Ed classes. Javier was humiliated and devastated, but said nothing.

Two nights later, Javier dressed himself in his father's military fatigues and took his father's rifle and a large hunting knife and went to battle. He broke into a darkened house and slashed every piece of furniture in the living room, before the single mother living in the home walked in, and then he shot her directly through the heart. She died immediately, leaving three little girls without a mother.

I asked Javier to explain his thinking when he set out on his fatal warpath that night.

"I couldn't please either of them," was his answer, referring to his mother and father.

"But, your mother seemed to stick up for you, didn't she?" I asked.

"You call that sticking up for me? She knew he'd beat the hell out of me if he ever found out I was learning to drive, so why did she let me? Did she like seeing me get beat?"

Although I already knew that the humiliation of being removed from the Drivers Ed classes was more devastating to Javier than the beating, I accepted his comment and asked why he had chosen to wear the military garb during his offense. He responded, "I was going to show him (his father) just who was the toughest—him or me. He always acted so tough when he wore that uniform. Do you know that he always wore military clothes in the house?"

Unfortunately, Javier's parents' inability to resolve their personal insecurities and marital conflicts, especially as related to their children's discipline, resulted in disaster. His parents' conflicting disciplinary styles confused him. This confusion resulted in his feeling unsafe with either parent. In his mind, his mother's permissiveness put him in the path of harm and his father's militant approach harmed him physically and devastated him emotionally. He could not trust either of his parents and therefore, he certainly did not feel he could safely talk to either of them about his feelings. He held his tongue as long as he was able and then ultimately made his own decision about how he could gain control over his own life.

My father would announce, before administering each spanking, "This is going to hurt me, more than it will hurt you." Do you think for one moment that I, as a child, ever believed him? Not on your life! Then I had children of my own and learned exactly how much it hurt him. Later, when I had children of others, I learned just how much it could hurt **them**.

We often hear the old refrain: "Spare the rod; spoil the child." The Bible verse from which that refrain is paraphrased, is actually much more emphatic: *"He that spareth the rod hateth his son: but he that loveth him chasteneth him betimes." — Proverbs 13:24.* Clearly, as loving parents, we will discipline our children. However, corporal punishment is a very complex matter.

Most parents are aware that physically disciplining a child has become a legal matter. Parents can be and actually are arrested and imprisoned for inflicting corporal punishment on their children. Often, when those parents are arrested for physical abuse of their children, their defense is to claim that the Bible, God's actual word, directed them to administer physical discipline to their child, espousing the refrain "spare the rod; spoil the child."

While I rarely mention it, I worked exactly one year for a child protective services unit, and saw first-hand the horrifying results of that abused refrain. There was the case of the three year old that is permanently blind and brain damaged. Her father said she would not stop crying, so he "slapped" her and shoved a garden hose down her throat and turned the water on full force, which according to his interpretation of the Bible was justified. I am still haunted by the vision of the last case I handled before saying, "enough is enough," and moving on to work in adoption. I will never forget that tiny two year old with two completely blackened eyes, totally swollen shut, below an enormous gauze turban—enormous not as a result of overuse of gauze, but because of the oversized swelling of his entire head—perhaps three sizes larger than the head of a normal two-year old. Tubes were inserted into every orifice of his unconscious body and machines pumped loudly to keep him alive. His mother couldn't get him to stay in bed, so she picked him up by his feet and whirled him around smacking his head repeatedly into the cold porcelain bathroom sink, and threw him to the tile floor. The Bible, she said, told her she must make her child obey. He died after three days on life support. Thus, I personally have great difficulty ever giving anyone reason to believe corporal punishment is justified for any reason, even by God's Word.

Years ago, advocates for making physical discipline illegal distributed a brochure, which also quoted the Bible, making reference to "sparing the rod." This brochure claimed that in biblical times, shepherds used "the rod" to prod their sheep, not to beat them to death. The brochure went on to say that while children obviously require discipline, using any device from hands to belts to I presume, garden hoses and bathroom sinks to administer any form of physical punishment was wrong and should be made illegal. Ultimately, they were successful in their quest.

Their brochure led me to reflect on something I remembered about a "rod" in the Bible. It was in the 23rd Psalm. I remembered it from my childhood, when we were actually instructed to repeat that Bible verse in school until it was thoroughly memorized! "The Lord is my shepherd… thy rod and thy staff shall comfort me."

Indeed! The rod mentioned here is a **comfort**, not an instrument of brutal lethality. This led to my belief that we are called to **comfort** our children with the same loving discipline the Lord uses to guide all of His children.

"Comforting discipline"! That has to be a contradiction in terms if I ever heard one; but in fact, children are comforted when parents establish clear boundaries for them. However, establishing those boundaries with physical pain does not seem to me to be comforting.

If we look at pictures of shepherds minding their flocks, we will note that most are leaning on their rods, using those rods to support and steady them on rocky terrain, rather than using them to discipline their sheep. When our children—our sheep—misbehave and lead us on rocky roads, it would seem to be the ultimate time for us to **lean** on a very strong rod for support rather than picking one up and using it as a tool to inflict pain on our child.

In most cases when God disciplines us, He **prods** us in the right direction. In my case, God has occasionally been known to use that little hook at the end of the shepherd's rod to tug me firmly back into line, stopping me from causing harm—to myself, or others, but never once has God used his rod to beat me into submission. His way is gentle. His discipline is comforting. Actually, His discipline is most often in the form of words. He communicates His discipline with the Word. He does not beat us over the head with it. In fact, most would agree that when someone uses His Word to beat us over the head, it rarely leads us in the direction they think we should go!

Most often a well-placed word will interrupt a behavior problem, should you be fortunate enough to catch your child in the actual act, as I did with Veronica in the spitting incident. Occasionally, it will be necessary to interrupt the behavior more firmly, by removing the child from the situation, as I did with Veronica. However, once the danger of physical harm to your child or others is long gone, it is time to enforce meaningful, comforting discipline. Then, using the Lord as a reference, forgive and forget the incident, and move ahead to continue building your loving relationship with your child.

Finding Common Ground

And the rain descended, and the floods came, and the winds blew, and beat upon that house and it fell not; for it was founded upon a rock. — *Matthew 7:25*

When a relationship is new and fresh, it seems easy to establish common ground. Early in relationships there do not seem to be the distractions that arise later. In adoption counseling, we called this "the honeymoon phase." Everything is intriguing. Each one is interested in what the other has to say. Each one wants to please the other. Somehow, there is time for each other. Special moments—an evening together, a walk in the park; visits with relatives, a concert or ball game, a summer vacation—all receive undivided attention. This is an exciting time. It is a time for establishing common ground.

Over time, maintaining that common ground becomes increasingly difficult. With time, warts begin to show. She takes forever to get dressed. He has to be asked ten times to take out the trash. The children interrupt every attempt at conversation. She spends too much time on the phone. He spends too much time working on the car. The kids turn the volume up on the TV—way too loud. She likes poodles. He wants a retriever. The kids want a collie. Energy is drained. Divisiveness sets in.

With time, responsibilities and obligations become overwhelming. Work demands increase, requiring more hours away from home. The kids start school—they have homework; dancing lessons; piano lessons; soccer practice; band rehearsal. Taxes need to be paid. She is asked to volunteer at the hospital and can't say "no." The car needs a new transmission. The neighbor needs Susie to baby-sit. The water heater goes out. Her friend is in the hospital and she needs to take care of her pets. He has to spend the morning paying the bills and balancing the checkbook. Johnny's invited to spend the night with a friend. Susie is off for a weekend retreat with the church group. Pulled in different directions at an amazing pace, common ground is crumbling. There is barely time to take care of what has to be done, let alone find time for what you want to do. There is certainly no time to come up with creative, fresh ideas to keep common ground fertile.

Initially, small clues tell you something is wrong. It is nothing you can put your finger on, so you brush the thoughts away plunging into new obligations, taking on more responsibilities. Unchecked, the clues become louder. He is working late every night of the week. She is heading up another PTA committee. Johnny has soccer practice twice this week, instead of once. Susie has nightly rehearsals for the school play. On and on it goes. Everyone is doing "his" thing and no longer is the family doing "our" thing. Crumbling common ground is falling away in clumps; it's heading for a landslide!

How do you stop a landslide single-handedly?

It's time for some FORESIGHT— Stop! Assess! Schedule! Plan!

So often we ignore the clues until we actually see the rubble of the landslide around our feet. We think—indeed even pray—the clues will evaporate. Unfortunately, problems do not resolve themselves. Without confrontation, what began as a small and insignificant dislodged pebble, becomes a huge tumbling boulder. The longer the problem is left unchecked, the greater it becomes. It is **not** going to go away. You either confront it at whatever point you discover it or let the boulders keep tumbling! No one can change the direction of the landslide but you!

Before the family fragments any further you must call for a "foresight pit stop" to assess how things became so unmanageable in your Parenting Business. You are the CEO—the leader. Assume the responsibility your role requires. Firmly, **make time** to call the family together. Take a deep breath and announce what you see happening to your family. Express your desire to have a close loving family. Ask what each one thinks needs to happen to re-establish that common ground you once enjoyed. Listen. Remember, it has taken some time to get to this point. The problem will not be resolved with one discussion. You can possibly develop small steps to begin the journey toward common ground.

At first it may only be possible to agree to disagree. Don't give up! You may be ready to move ahead with a commitment and a plan, however, for others in the family it will be a new idea. It will require an entire change in thinking. It will be necessary to revisit your plan as many times as necessary to bring your family back to solid ground.

We have come full circle. Once again you must commit to "work" on relationships. This means giving up some of the responsibilities and obligations that are cluttering divisive schedules. This means saying "no" to new responsibilities and obligations that come your way.

Start small. In our whirling fast food society, this means scheduling. Perhaps your family will resist having dinner together every night of the week. However, you may be able to lead them to commit fully to a sliver of **unequivocal, uninterrupted** time for the family. It may be one hour a week. It may begin with only one meal each *month*. Whatever time frame they will agree to, no one makes other plans. It is written boldly on all calendars and announced to family, friends and co-workers that at this one time, you are **not available**. It is up to you, as the leader, to set the example. You must commit to remaining adamant about family time. It is the only way it will happen. It is this commitment to an unequivocally, uninterrupted sliver of time, that will make a huge difference in the direction your family is headed.

With crumbling common ground, one might forget how it was ever solidified in the first place.

Solidifying
Common Ground

And thou shalt love the Lord thy God with all thy heart and with all thy soul and with all thy might. And these words, which I command thee this day, shall be in thine heart: And thou shalt teach them diligently unto thy children, and shalt talk of them when thou sittest in thine house, and when thou walkest by the way and when thou liest down, and when thou risest up. And thou shalt bind them for a sign upon thine hand, and they shall be as frontlets between thine eyes. And thou shalt write them upon the posts of thy house and on thy gates. — Deuteronomy 6:5-9

As I write, I am beginning to realize it might sound as though I think I have "all the answers." I wish I did. If I had "all" the answers, we could eradicate prisons and mental health facilities, guidance centers, divorce courts and the like. Unfortunately, I only think I may have some answers for some people.

What I am writing, I only know from 20/20 hindsight. If I had only known these things when I began raising my family, I would have done things oh, so differently. While I am grateful for the closeness we now share as a family, I now know it could have come earlier and much more easily, had I known where to find even some of the answers. I just wish I could find a "Procedures Manual" for "in-lawing" or "grand-parenting." I've been looking! Undoubtedly, I will make many mistakes and all of us will experience many more bumps and bruises on the road to gathering 20/20 hindsight for our new roles!

So, when I suggest activities for solidifying common ground in your family you should know that our family only engaged in a few. Others I have learned from friends, co-workers, reading, etc., far after the fact; hence the 20/20 hindsight. Many of them would have been beneficial to our struggling family. Of course, not all activities will work for all families, so while I am sure we would have tried many had we thought of them, there are some that would not have worked for us, but may work for you.

Get cooking, together!

I recently phoned my daughter, Melissa, reaching her on her cell phone while she was baby-sitting for a friend. In the background I heard a tiny voice begging her, "I wanna make pea-budder cookies."

Over and over I heard the refrain. Finally, I asked her, "What's he saying?"

"Oh! He wants me to make peanut butter cookies with him. He helps his mother measure ingredients when she's making his favorite cookies. He's learning numbers and fractions. He's only three!"

Three years old, and he's actually learning fractions in the kitchen!

I was reminded of how I dreaded letting my children in the kitchen when they were small. It's dangerous, and, besides, they'd make a huge mess!

Suddenly, I realized what a privilege I missed to "teach" my children right in my kitchen. What a waste of precious time—time I could have used to build our relationships. But, no, I was busy shooing them away!

Encourage your children of a reasonable-reasoning age to join you in the kitchen, as you assure that they are safely away from heat sources, open flames and sharp items. Even very young children can safely pour, stir and help with clean up. It's an opportunity for them to learn about responsibility.

On those nights you rent a video for the family to watch together, don't send one member off into the kitchen to pop popcorn alone—do it together as a family! As you decide who pours, who pops, who salts or who butters, you are building common ground by noting that each family member is equally important to the project—equally important to the family. Do it together, it's family-night, after all!

Cook up non-food concoctions, too! There are recipes for play dough and bubbles. Remember salt maps? Map out your summer vacation in the gooey substance! Get creative—then play with the results, together!

Not only is this an opportunity for the family to come together, adults can also learn a great deal from children. They are not constrained by the same rules as adults. They will innovate and create, if we allow their minds to imagine. Their "take" on an old recipe may result in something fabulous, or it will teach them something about following instructions. In either case, they will learn and so will you.

Ride a city bus, together!

Whether you always ride the city bus or have never set foot on one, this may give you a new perspective on an old means of transportation.

Bob had rather modest beginnings, but he had done well for himself as an adult. He was especially pleased to have an administrative position and looked forward to going to work each day. When the company came upon hard times and closed, Bob found himself living on unemployment, unable to find a similar position. Although he questioned this turn of fortune, he maintained faith that he would eventually find a similar position. In the meantime, he took a rather menial position at my parents' store.

With his generous salary gone, Bob was unable to maintain the payment of his bills. When his car was repossessed, he was forced to ride the city bus. Day after day Bob had interesting stories to tell about his ride to work on the bus. Some days it was his realization of the struggle many people have with poverty, forcing their dependence on others. Those were usually the days the bus was late, broken down, or the bus driver was less than polite. On other days he reported noticing sites that had always been there, but he never had time to see when driving his car. On yet other days, he had uplifting stories about conversations with other bus riders.

One morning an elderly woman took a seat next to him at the bus stop. He was especially discouraged that day, having received a notice from the apartment manager, because he was behind on his rent. He knew he was not going to be able to maintain his prized apartment for long. Although Bob only smiled and said a polite, "Good morning" to the woman, she seemed intent on engaging him in conversation.

The eighty-one year old woman told Bob she went every day by bus to visit sick and elderly people, who could not leave their homes. She would pray with them, bringing them hope, a little pleasure and occasionally something she had baked in her kitchen.

Although Bob had not told her anything about himself, "out of the blue" she told him she knew he was in a great deal of pain now, but he would once again "see the sunshine." She shared her faith with Bob right there at the bus stop, and then asked if she could pray with him.

With tears welling up in his eyes, Bob said that as the woman prayed he began to acknowledge a true need to turn to God with his situation. He then made a statement about not buying a car again. He said his experiences while riding the bus were too valuable to miss.

Whether or not you have your own transportation, riding the bus can be an enriching experience. If you generally ride the city bus, use the time in a new way. Get a new perspective on things. Change your traditional seat from the front to the back, or left to the right. Don't read. Smile at strangers! Take a risk and get acquainted. Do things differently.

If you are new to bus riding, your family may find similar uplifting experiences, or you may simply see your town from a new perspective. New perspectives bring new awareness. You will certainly have time to get to know one another as you experience new adventures together.

Complete a family project, together!

One fond memory for our family came not so very long ago. My oldest daughter decided to coordinate our family in an effort to fix up my parents' house. While the effort involved replacing a few large portions of rotten boards and painting the entire house, the work was made much lighter by joining together and making it a time of family togetherness. Several creative painting techniques were inspired by a good deal of chatter and laughter, and the job was done!

Together as a family, improve your home, simplify, beautify or generally enhance your lifestyle. Here are some ideas that may work for your family.

- Wash the car together—everyone gets wet!
- Reorganize a catchall closet or junk drawer.

- Clean out the garage—then hold a garage sale, together.
- Recycle together—it becomes everyone's responsibility to save our earth.
- Paint a room, together—be creative and chatter and laugh a lot.
- Shampoo or groom the dog, together.
- Finally, put those photos in albums and reminisce, together.
- Have a shoe-polishing day—polish someone else's shoes.
- Together, finish off the attic or garage for a family game area, where you can spend more time together.
- Gather items that have been unused for one year—give them away, together.
- Together, plant bulbs for Spring beauty or plant seeds and watch them bloom all summer and into autumn.
- Plant a tree in honor of a special person or significant event, together.

Work does not have to be drudgery. Make washing the car or improving your home fun, not punishment. This is not to say that every family project must be joyful. It is critical to instill in children the importance of responsible, serious work. Not everything in life is a party. Some things just have to get done, whether we like it or not. However, for the purpose of building common ground, just have fun!

Adopt a family pet, together!

Solidify common ground with a pet. Not only are pets a source of unconditional love, they help children understand compassion and caring while learning responsibility. Pets also provide a source for children to understand the cycle of life.

Be sure the pet fits your family lifestyle. As a family, read up on pet care requirements for different types of pets. Together, decide which pet will become a new "family member." Together, go to the pound or pet shop. Check the newspaper for animals for sale or give-away. Together, go to meet the pet. Then—plan a family pet-care routine that will incorporate everyone. Teach the bird to talk, together. Walk the dog, together. Clean out the fish tank or birdcage, together. Not only does sharing the responsibility make the job lighter, it is an opportunity to enjoy each other's company and build common ground.

Create, together!

One recent Christmas I found an especially nice book filled with craft ideas to do with children. I wrapped it as a gift for my daughter-in-law. She enjoys crafting with the children, and is always looking for new ideas. The next time I saw the book it was placed among the cookbooks on the kitchen counter—a virtual "staple" for kitchen activities with the kids! There are numerous craft activity books with hundreds of activities to do with children of all ages. Helping stimulate your child's imagination will do wonders for your own! You might become so creative that your family may even come up with its own new creative craft ideas—and you can write your own book—together!

Schedule a regular family playtime, together!

"Play" is actually a child's "work." Routine childhood play is critical to a child's mental, emotional, social and physical development. More specifically, play is the means by which children learn critical life skills. Through play, children develop:
- Problem solving skills
- Communication skills
- A sense of fairness
- An understanding and acceptance of rules and boundaries
- Leadership skills
- "Follower-ship" skills
- A healthy imagination
- A creative spirit
- An ability to win proudly and humbly
- An ability to lose graciously, without losing face
- Social skills
- Friendships

As important as play is for children, it is equally as important for adults. Because of our busy schedules, we often omit playtime to save time. Don't! Play is vital to the emotional health and welfare of your entire family, and that includes you!

Observing an afternoon treatment group at the juvenile facility one day, I heard the following description of how these kids played.

"Well, in our 'hood' we played this game. We wrapped our legs in

towels and shot pellets into each other's legs. Whoever got the most pellets in the towel, won!"

Another youth responded, "Well, in our 'hood' we didn't use towels"

"Yee gads!" I thought to myself. "These kids absolutely have to learn what it means to play."

Several weeks before, for no apparent reason, I purchased several dozen bottles of bubbles on sale at the local Wal-Mart. I stashed them in a building we used for art therapy groups, way across campus. In a flash, I stood up and told the boys, "Follow me."

I know the dorm staff thought I was crazy when, like a mother duck I broke protocol and marched a row of twenty-five ducklings out of the building and across the campus. I unlocked the door to the small building and herded the ducklings inside.

I don't deny feeling some trepidation as I sat the street-smart boys on the floor of the barren room, and went to the storage cabinet to retrieve two large brown paper bags. I thought to myself, "God only knows what they are going to do when they see these bubbles!" I took a deep breath and silently prayed, "Please God, let this work and don't let them say, 'Hey! We're not babies!'"

I took the bags into the room of twenty-five pretty tough looking young men, most much bigger than me. Holding one bag out, I told the first boy to reach in and grab whatever he felt. He looked up at me for a moment, and then gingerly reached into the bag I was holding just above his head. He pulled out a bottle of bubbles and stared at me. Then he smiled, as the others began chirping, "Bubbles! She's got bubbles! Hey, man! It's bubbles!" You would have thought I was handing out gold nuggets!

For the next forty minutes these street-smart young men blew bubbles without ceasing. They filled the entire room with bubbles. We went outside and they whirled with bubbles. They made up games with bubbles. They blew bubbles on each other. They blew bubbles on me! Bubbles filled the air over the campus and so did their shouts of glee!

When it was time to return to the dorm, each boy carefully capped his remaining bubbles and quietly placed their bottle back into the brown paper bags. With the exception of a few questions about when we could do this again, there was silence. I led the group back to their dorm, leaving them with their thoughts.

After that, I knew that play must become an integral part of their treatment. Play had obviously been a developmental milestone that was missing in most of their lives. Subsequently, with our dorm treatment staff, I developed a program that allowed the youth to earn the privilege of playing. As the youth achieved their fifth and highest behavioral level, they were awarded with a once a month "fun night," as long as they maintained that level. Many of our activities involved playing with children's toys: hula-hoops, bubbles, jacks, jump ropes, nerf balls and such. It was delightful to see them retrieve a milestone most of them had missed.

On very special occasions we were able to take these highest-level youth off campus. With a herd of staff almost equaling the number of youth, we loaded into vans and went off to places where we could play. While many dorms took their youth to movies, I refused. I just could not comprehend the relevance of sitting silently in the dark for two hours, as anything resembling useful.

Our dorms went roller-skating. Few of the youth had ever had skates on their feet before. We went bowling. They couldn't figure out how to get their fingers in the holes. Once we went to a traveling circus. None of the kids in our group had ever been to a circus before.

However, the highlight of all outings had to be our Christmas outings. The maximum-security facility was located at the edge of town, bordered by vast stretches of open ranch land. One of the nearby ranchers had a wonderful tradition. He and his family created a Christmas fantasyland in their fields. Each year this Christmas project grew, as they created and built new, lighted displays. They hooked a flatbed trailer to the back of a pick-up, lined it with bales of hay and took visitors on hayrides through their fantasyland of lighted displays.

The hayride was followed with a hot dog roast and sing-a-long and occasionally charades, around a huge roaring campfire. At the hundred-year-old farmhouse on their property, the family served wassail and cookies and visitors could play checkers on handmade oversized checkerboards, or just sit in large wooden rocking chairs on the porch. On a clear, cold night every star could be seen individually shining brightly against the black sky.

Believing these youth needed the fullness of the campfire experience; I brought marshmallows to roast along with the hot dogs. That evening, we had more youth qualified to go with us than I realized, and I was concerned that we would run out of marshmallows before everyone had a chance to roast theirs. I gave one large bag of marshmallows to Michael, one most trusted youth, to "hide" under his extra-large jacket, until we were sure everyone had their chance.

As we were nearing the end of our wonderful evening, the rancher came up to me carrying an enormous bag and asked if the kids would like to roast more marshmallows. He said they wouldn't need them any more that year, since this was their last tour of the Christmas season. I looked at this commercial sized bag of marshmallows and thought about stomachaches. But, this was a special occasion. I thanked him and we passed the bag around the campfire.

The kids were quiet, engrossed in watching marshmallow-blue flames on the ends of four foot long fork tines. In the silence, I heard a "plop." Then I heard one of the staff shout, "Hey!" I heard another, "plop" as I saw the staff member watch a white marshmallow roll off his shoulder, down the front of his bright red shirt, landing at his feet. He picked up the marshmallow and said sternly, "Who threw this?" There was no response.

I looked around the circle of boys encompassing the campfire. There sat Michael with a Cheshire grin. I watched as he stealthily withdrew a soft white marshmallow from the forgotten bag of marshmallows under his jacket and he threw it firmly across the fire.

Suddenly, the whole group—staff and youth alike—were on their feet, chasing each other, tagging each other with marshmallows. Marshmallows were flying. Feet were flying. Round and round the old farmhouse they chased. Marshmallows were plopping on heads and chests and backs. Laughter filled the air.

When I saw the rancher walking toward me, I abruptly stopped playing the game, but the staff and youth continued. I had visions of being required to pick up each and every marshmallow we'd tossed. With the shouts and laughter continuing in the background, the rancher said to me, "I've been doing this for a long, long time—probably longer than you've been alive. We've had all kinds of groups out here, and I want to tell you, we've never seen any group of people—old or young—have as much fun as these folks are having here tonight. It does my heart good to see their absolute joy!"

I couldn't respond, as I pushed back tears. I thought, "God. Thank you for making the bubbles work. Let them always remember the joy of that playful child within. And, please God, let them know You are the source of their true joy."

Tour your hometown, together!

I raised my children in San Antonio, a city that derives much of its economic resources from tourism. However, I frequently heard local people say they had not been to the Riverwalk since they were children, or they had never been to the Alamo! While they would travel far for vacations, they never thought of taking a trip downtown to see the sights. That irony brings to mind a story I put together to help the youth at the juvenile facility gain an understanding that the grass is not always greener on the other side of the street.

An old couple sat rocking on their front porch, bemoaning their fate in life. "Why, Oh why are we so poor? Why have we been forced to struggle for every cent? Why in our old age must we struggle just to put food on the table?"

One day a young man came up to them on the porch and told them he was searching for a lost diamond mine. He said an old map he found led him right to their home. The map indicated they were literally sitting on a diamond mine.

The old couple angrily told the young man, "If we were sitting on a diamond mine, do you think we would be living in this shabby old house?"

The young man smiled and told them that if they would let him excavate their property, he would gladly share his findings with them, fifty-fifty. He held out a paper indicating this agreement in writing.

The old man grabbed the paper, looked it over and tore it into shreds. He told the young man, "Go dig. If you find diamonds, keep 'em. But, even I know fifty percent of nothing is still nothing."

The young man returned the next day. He asked again for written permission to begin excavating the old couple's property. Again, he told them he would share his findings. The old man signed the agreement. Scratching out the fifty-fifty clause, he wrote a big zero in its place.

The young man dragged his tools into their backyard. For days and weeks he dug and scraped away at the soil.

The old couple sat on their front porch, mocking and laughing at the young man's efforts. They continued bemoaning their own fate in life.

One day the young man walked around to the front porch. He said, "You know, you were right. There are no diamonds back there, the map must have been wrong." He held out a small bag and handed it to the old couple. The old couple peered inside the bag. As the young man took back his small bag and began walking away, he shouted to the old couple, "You were right. The map was wrong, there are no diamonds, but there is gold!"

Simply put, we may be sitting on a gold mine and not know it. Look around. What treasures are in your backyard that you have not taken time to appreciate and enjoy?

Your city may not have the profusion of tourist sites San Antonio holds, but undoubtedly there are places of interest that may be enriching. Use your phone book as a guide to hidden treasures in your town. Check with your Chamber of Commerce. Drop by a motel and check for pamphlets about tourist sites in and around your area. Have your entire family mine for gold in their own backyard.

Organize a neighborhood get-together, together!

Lead your family in initiating a neighborhood barbecue or pot-luck supper.

There doesn't have to be a special occasion. Although, it could be an opportunity to welcome new neighbors, celebrate a victory or share the excitement of the birth of a neighbor's new baby—or grandchild! It could be an opportunity to celebrate a neighbor's new car, or the addition of a pet to their family. Look for reasons to celebrate, and then organize!

Talk to your neighbors together. Form neighborhood committees. Get as many of your neighbors as actively involved with your family as possible.

Your efforts might lead to a neighborhood action group—Neighborhood Watch; Beautify Our Neighborhood, etc., or they may simply provide opportunities to know your family and your neighbors better.

Become inventors, together!

Some of my most rewarding experiences in counseling have been those rare opportunities to observe families and other groups I've worked with actually put into practice the skills gained from our sessions. One activity provided opportunities for me to simply observe. Those performing the activity were often so totally focused on just having fun together, they forgot I was even in the room!

This activity is an opportunity for us "pack-rats" to put to use some of those items that have just been waiting for a "someday we might need this" moment. Use all that junk to invent a family game!

Randomly gather junk from the junk drawer or other hidden junk stashes in your home. You need only five to ten pieces of junk—lids, cans, Styrofoam containers, string, paper towel or toilet paper cores, bottle caps, bent paper clips, broken or mismatched items and the like. Put them on the table, then as a family create a game with them. Make your own rules. Be sure everyone in the family is capable of playing by those rules, and then play it! Have fun refining the game or gather a new selection of junk and create a totally new game each time you play! The prize for winning; a big family HUG!

Become encouragers, together!

Attend a special event in which no family member is involved, together!

Take the family to any sports event, just for the pure enjoyment of it. Munch on hot dogs and cheer for the team. It may be a local high school ball game or a neighbor child's peewee league game your family attends together! Attend some sports event you've never experienced before—polo, swimming, golf, tennis, auto racing, etc. The idea is to attend totally stress free, because you aren't invested in who wins!

Perhaps a neighbor's child is having a recital. Take your family to show support! Clap loudly. Be lavish with praise. Coordinate a special treat for the child after the recital—ice cream sundae construction in your kitchen might be fun! Go just for the fun of it! It's not all about winning or losing or how gracefully or melodically the child performs. It's how your family, together cheers on the players and performers, that really counts!

Form a family investment club, together!

If there were a "Parenting Handbook of Life," under the heading of "Building Economic Responsibility in Children" there should be a section marked "Understanding Economic Principles."

At the end of visitors' day, I was supervising several young men who were cleaning up the visiting area at the maximum-security facility. As they swept litter from the back of the room to where I was standing near the door, I heard tinkling sounds. I asked them to check what they were sweeping out.

"It ain't nothin' Miss. Just a bunch of pennies," and they just kept on sweeping.

Nothing, indeed! We had a lesson in economic principles right there!

Children see adults writing something on a colorful piece of paper and exchanging it for goods at the store. They watch as we hand a piece of plastic to the store clerk. She runs it through a fancy machine and then says, "Thank you," as she hands us our goods. They note when we take out a wad of green paper and exchange it for items at the store. The principles behind those pieces of paper or plastic are sometimes never learned. Children grow up to be adults who still say, "Just write a check;" "Just charge it, if you want it!"

Take time each week to collect all the change in your house—pennies included! Have the children participate by checking pockets, under cushions and the car seat, anywhere loose change may have fallen. Set up a container and begin dropping in the coins your family finds. When you have collected a sufficient amount, as a family, take your collection to the neighborhood bank and set up a special savings account. Review the bank statements together, and help the children learn the principle of interest. As a family, decide how the money will be used. Perhaps it will become a family vacation fund, or family night out fund, or a fund for a special Christmas gift for the entire family or you may want to make it a donation fund for your favorite charity.

You might pick a stock to follow, whether you actually invest or not. A budget might be more appealing, if all family members are involved in maintaining it. Let the whole family participate in balancing the family checkbook. Review charge account bills together, explaining the interest charges for not paying on time or not paying your full balance. Explain, explain, explain! Teaching children the value of pennies will result in their respect for dollars.

Many parents do not share financial difficulties with each other, let alone their children. Perhaps this secrecy is due to embarrassment, or simply because they do not believe their children, or even their partner, will understand the complexity of the situation. When financial difficulties hit your family, it is a critical time for all to pull together as one, to resolve the problem. This can only happen by sharing the truth of the matter.

Allen wondered why his father was still at home when he left for school each morning. His father had worked for the same company for almost fifteen years, and left the house every morning at six o'clock precisely. Now, at seven-thirty he was still in pajamas, drinking coffee in the kitchen as Allen was leaving for school.

When neither of his parents commented on Allen's father being home in the mornings, Allen decided his father must be sick. At dinner one night he asked if his father was having surgery, or something. His parents looked at each other and then at Allen, but neither answered the question.

Allen was very disturbed by his parents' sudden secrecy. Suddenly, his usually good grades plunged. He began staying out very late, even on school nights. His parents tried to talk to him about the changes in his behavior, but he shrugged them off.

One evening almost six months after the secrecy began, the doorbell rang and Allen's father went to the door. A policeman asked whether Allen was home. His father said, "No," and asked what the problem was. The policeman informed Allen's parents that their son had been identified in the robbery of a convenience store in which an employee and customer were killed.

Allen's parents were stunned. Their bright, carefree child could not possibly have had anything to do with such an atrocity. They always closely monitored his friends, they always knew where he was going; they assured he did his homework. What more could parents do?

When Allen's mother took the stand to plead for mercy in the punishment phase of his trial, she wept as she told how her husband had been laid-off from his job and had been unable to find work. She sobbed as she begged the jury to allow Allen to return home on probation to help the family in these troubled financial times.

Of course, the jury was not lenient. Allen was found to be the leader of a group of boys who were stealing, simply for the "fun of it." They just thought it would be exciting to hold up the convenience store. Allen had encouraged one of the boys to bring his father's gun that night. Allen held the gun, while the other boys ransacked the store. They stole candy, chips, gum and soda. When Allen thought the clerk was going to push the alarm, he panicked and began wildly shooting the gun, resulting in taking two very innocent lives.

When Allen arrived at the youth facility, he was sullen. It was many months before he could talk about his crime openly. When he finally started talking about his behavior and incarceration, his greatest rage was at the fact that his parents had not trusted him enough to tell him about their financial difficulty. He was enraged that he only learned of it in the courtroom.

Was this tragedy necessary? Would it even have been conceived, if Allen's parents had simply told him the truth? Regardless, what was wrong with the truth? Of course, not every failure to tell our children the difficulties of our lives will end in such an enormous tragedy. However, is it ever necessary to be less than truthful with our children? You may be able to think of occasions the truth is wrong, but I cannot. I know children's imaginations, like most of ours, conjure up fantasies far worse than the truth could ever be.

I recall once counseling with a young man who was obviously withholding some very painful, deep, dark secret. After a number of sessions, with this apparent roadblock, I told him that since he would not share this secret with me, all I could do was make up what I would consider to be the worst thing that might have happened to him. Then I said, "So, since you won't tell me, I have to imagine that the worst thing I can imagine that would have happened to you is that you were sexually abused."

He bolted out of his chair and shouted, "No! It's nothing like that! It's just that my parents got divorced and I never saw my father again. It must have been my fault he left! He must hate me."

"Well, you see," I told him, "Your 'worst' and my 'worst' are very different. If we want to understand each other we have to be honest, and we have to tell each other what is really bothering us. To me, being sexually abused would be the worst thing. To you, your father's leaving the family is the worst."

To parents "the worst" may be losing a job, getting too deep into debt or squandering the family fortune. To your child, "the worst" probably has nothing to do with anything closely related to your finances.

When I finally had the opportunity to meet with Allen's parents, I asked them why they had not shared their financial difficulties with him. His mother noted, "We had promised him a car for his

*seventeenth birthday. He had his heart set on that car." Allen's dad
added, "Now, we weren't going to be able to come through for him, and
it was all my fault."*

*I said to his parents, "You thought the worst thing Allen could
experience was your not getting him a car?" I turned to Allen and
said, "Allen, why don't you share with your parents what your worst
thoughts were."*

*Allen looked squarely at his father and solemnly related, "I thought
you were dying."*

Our society so emphasizes money as the prime worth of a man,
that loss of money becomes paralyzing. When we equate our own
worth with material possessions, we often miss the true treasures
that can never be taken away. While our financial situation may not
be something for public disclosure, sharing it as a family brings opportunities for mutual support and encouragement—opportunities
necessary for building common ground.

Take a nature hike, together!

Head for a park or a nature trail and just enjoy listening for birds
and watching nature, together as a family. Take your bikes and make
it a "bike-hike"! Take your cameras and make it a "photo safari"!
Make a list of things you would like to see: specific rocks; leaves;
flowers; bugs; animals, etc., and make it a "nature scavenger hunt."
Long walks offer excellent opportunities for long talks! Long talks
build common ground.

Take an old fashioned Sunday drive, together!

Take the family for a drive around a special neighborhood or a
new subdivision in your town. Head out to the country or a neigh-
boring town. Remember to talk to each other about what you see.

A ride in the car is a good time for a heart to heart discussion. It
is not an opportunity to kidnap your children and force them to talk
to you or to hear what you have to say. It is an opportunity to develop
common ground by engaging in a non-threatening, supportive conversation about something that needs to be discussed—or just to get
to know each other better.

There was recently a series of powerful public service ads on television. Parents are folding laundry with their child; eating with their

child; riding in the car with their child, and no one utters a single word. At the end, a printed message flashes on the screen: "Another missed opportunity to talk to your child about drugs." A more generic message might have been just as powerful: "Another missed opportunity to get to know your child." I would then add, "...and, another missed opportunity for children to get to know their parents."

Although my children were quite young at the time their father and I divorced, I knew I had to tell them something. Their whole life had been disrupted, and despite their young ages, I knew they had questions. There were so many distractions in the house that I decided to load them all in the car and take them for a drive.

We didn't go very far. At that time we lived in the country and drives around our neighborhood most often became adventures. It wasn't long before we spied several deer. I stopped the car and we sat silently staring at the deer, which obliged us by staring back for a lengthy period. I had no idea what to say as I began haltingly recounting the fact that mommy and daddy would not be living together any more. I tried to be reassuring that they would spend time with Daddy and that above all, we both loved them dearly. We sat only briefly talking and listening, however that brief car ride was apparently one of the better ideas I stumbled on as a floundering parent.

Years later the older children have recounted that car ride, and especially remember that they were assured the divorce was in no way their fault and that they were given permission to love both of their parents. The long lasting effects of that car ride let me know that spending time with our children, totally free of distraction, is critical to the emotional health and welfare of a family.

Why, when we're standing side by side with our children for lengthy periods, can it be so difficult to find anything to talk about?

It is because we have no common ground.

We live together with our children for a lifetime, and yet know little about one another. We are so distracted and emotionally distanced from one another; we struggle to even make small talk. Taking that first step is very difficult, but so very important in building and maintaining intimacy in our relationships.

Fill your family drives with small talk to build common ground. Once common ground is established, the heart to heart rides will come.

Roam flea markets and garage sales, together!

One of the things I may have done right as a parent was to take my children to flea markets and garage sales. I wish I could say that I planned these outings solely for the benefit of my children. Unfortunately, my motives were somewhat selfish. Hunting for treasures amongst masses of junk was, and is, one of my passions. However, what started with less than honorable intentions became a wonderful experience for us all.

The people manning their booths seemed to enjoy sharing the history of their items with my children. I began encouraging them to ask about unusual items. Not only were they learning something about history in a fun manner, they were developing social and communication skills. As flea markets became very commercial, I began taking the children to antique shops. We especially looked for the "junky" kind. The children never hesitated to approach the shopkeeper to ask questions about interesting items.

We also scoured garage sales, finding truth in the saying, "One man's junk is another man's treasure!" Indeed, much of my home is furnished with such treasures! Not all that long ago, I shared in my daughter's excitement when she phoned, long distance, to announce that she had found a wonderful old trunk next to garbage piled by the street! Oh, the simple pleasures of life!

As a result of all this treasure hunting, my children also developed some beneficial economic principles. They learned to appreciate quality, especially in handcrafted items. They recognize value in purchasing. Further, my children all have an appreciation for the past. They are the ones in our family who are gathering historical information on the family. They know well, how to save their pennies for something they really want; and signs and symbols relating to our treasure hunting adventures bring back fond, loving and fun-filled memories for all of us.

At a recent family gathering we all piled in the car to visit an old house we lived in when the children were very young. While traveling around our old neighborhood we saw a sign. In unison they all yelled out, "Mom! Stop! Estate Sale!" The car screeched to a halt, we piled out and spent an hour pouring over old items, giggling and reminiscing. It was like the "old days." What wonderful shared memories!

Plant a vegetable garden, together!

A truly economical family activity is to plan, prepare and plant ·
a vegetable garden, together. Everyone can participate in tending the
garden, watching it flourish and harvesting the bountiful crop. Take
it a step further and get everyone involved in cooking, canning and
preserving the produce.

If there is excess, give the produce to a homeless shelter or other
worthy cause you select together as a family. Pack it up and deliver
it, together.

If you aren't fortunate enough to have an area for gardening, seek
out a community garden in your city. Often your county extension
office will host a garden for people in the community to share. On
a common piece of property, you plant your own garden and have
the privilege of sharing your produce with others. They also share
their produce with you. If your area does not have such a community project, perhaps your family will be the one to encourage your
county extension office to start one.

If no garden plot is available, your family might research culti-
vating a garden in pots on a terrace or patio.

Adding a few flowers to the garden is cheerful touch! Pick them
and cheer friends and family with gifts of flowers all summer long!

Play old-fashioned board games and work puzzles, together!

Get out the card table! Set it up in a rarely used area and put together old fashioned, cardboard picture puzzles. Make space to play
board games together.

In this day of fast paced electronic entertainment, note that any
game you play on your computer or at an arcade actually *barricades*
opportunities for conversation. A few "I got ya's" or "I'm gonna blast
you off the screen's," but nothing meaningful. Be concerned if your
children, or you for that matter, become mesmerized in cyber-space
for hours on end. While electronic gizmos have improved our lives
in many ways, they have also eroded our personal connections.

I love e-mail. I must check my e-mail ten times a day. However,
I now have several out of town friends I haven't talked to in person
for months, because we "talk" daily via a TV screen. I love our daily

"TV-chats," but wonder at times how electronic connections have affected our relationship.

You may remember comic books from years ago, showing that our society had become a mass of huge heads propped on shelves in front of mesmerizing television-like screens. What was once science fiction in comic books has, all too often, become reality. Is that where we're headed now, giant heads interacting with TV monitors?

Encourage your children to interact with people—real flesh and blood human people. Play games that encourage communication and personal interaction. That is the only way to build common ground!

Develop a family hobby, together!

Look for interests that seem prevalent in your family—or could, given a little prompting. It might be photography, stamp or coin collecting, bird watching or learning magic tricks—put on shows for family and friends. There may be an interest in woodworking that could be coupled with another interest in tole painting or stenciling. Perhaps, repair toys together to give to needy children—especially as an annual family Christmas project. The more mechanically minded family members assemble and the artsy ones paint and decorate the finished product! Look for other complimentary interests that may be linked together as a satisfying family hobby.

Remember, the importance of doing the project together is to use the time to communicate and get to know one another—you are building common ground!

Visit the library, together!

Local libraries abound with resources far beyond books alone. There are magazines, newspapers, videos, recordings, even artwork for loan and a whole host of activities, especially for children. Pack up the family and travel to libraries outside of your neighborhood, just for a new perspective.

Observe family members for different interests, as each wanders to a favorite section of the library. On the drive home, talk about the differences you observe. Encourage sharing those diverse interests to enrich one another.

The interests you observe may be important clues to underlying thoughts and feelings. With all the concern about what is affecting children's behavior these days, it is prudent to purposely watch for patterns in your children's interests. From the youngest age, as your child begs you to read bedtime stories, patterns become evident. When you observe potentially problematic patterns you have an opportunity to redirect inclinations about which you have concerns.

When should you begin to be concerned?

Trust your instincts. Then look for concrete clues.

Is your child frequently or only asking you to read aggressive or frightening stories? Are stories about kindness, responsibility and hope almost always ignored or rejected altogether? Is this pattern similar with TV and other interests?

If you are unsure about a pattern, ask your child questions to clarify his interests. After reading a favorite story, ask, "Tell me your favorite part of that story?" After observing a rough interaction with a peer, ask, "What is it you enjoy most about playing with Tommy?" Does your child frequently report that the hostile, aggressive or dangerous aspects are what they enjoy?

Ask your child to make up a story to tell you. NOTE: It is very important not to react to the story, until it is completed. Remember the principles of remaining objective and non-judgmental? If you indicate your own feelings, whether approval or disapproval, the child's true thoughts and feelings will go underground.

Is the story filled with aggression, violence, and unkind or hurtful comments?

You may wonder: If your child frequently engages in aggressive activities, but also often shows a great deal of compassion, shouldn't one counteract the other?

The answer is that no person is all good or all bad. In my professional experience I came to believe the term "hardened criminals" should actually be, "petrified marshmallows." Of the hundreds of adult and youth offenders I've known, I never met one who did not have a soft spot. In fact, it often seemed the tougher the exterior, the softer the marshmallow inside.

Larry murdered an eighty-year-old woman, then raped her and sat on her body as he ate from her refrigerator. Can you think of a more horrendously brutal, sadistically disgusting, violent crime? While confined, Larry remained violent. A physically huge sixteen-year-old, he pummeled his peers, splintered furniture and once smashed a double strength plate glass with his fist. With blood pouring from his arm he warned others, "Watch out! Be careful! You'll get cut on the broken glass!'

Larry was the first person on the scene to help when another person was hurting. He was the first to warn peers that they were getting themselves in trouble and to give positive advice to think before they acted. He became tearful at the sight of a dead bird lying alongside the sidewalk.

Ronnie coldly accepted eighty dollars to murder the parents of a classmate he hardly knew. He walked into the house, shot the boy's parents to death and walked out. He never showed a glimmer of remorse. While in confinement he stole, he lied, and occasionally assaulted peers. Ronnie was actually the first person I ever met that I thought might be "without a conscience."

Yet, Ronnie was capable of volunteering to serve as a human crutch for a peer who had injured his ankle in a basketball game. He shouldered his peer up a hill the distance of a football field to get him to the infirmary. He was capable of cuddling kittens that had been dumped off on the deserted country road, and had found their way into the trash bin by the dorm. He could smile; he could carry on a meaningful conversation. While I still doubt he has a conscience, he exhibited human emotions of care and concern.

The examples are endless, however, the theme remains the same. It is not only possible, but also highly likely, that the most heinous of cold, calculating criminals is very capable of having and exhibiting the most sensitive human emotions of care and concern. Therefore, we cannot rule out danger simply because we observe kindness accompanying aggressiveness. We must address the aggressiveness.

What we can do is maintain vigilance. Be observant for clues indicating a problem. Listen to comments. The seemingly most innocent comment may provide the biggest clue. When there is a clue evident, remove all blinders, push through all fears and plunge headlong into the resolution of the concern. While you are using family activities to enjoy one another and create opportunities to build common ground, these activities serve as ideal tools for assessing difficulties. Once assessed, set your action plan into immediate motion. Don't sweep concerns under the carpet; face them boldly, as you would face any roaring lion.

Visit local museums and art galleries, together!

A fine way to build common ground is to let your children see you learning right alongside them. As you see new museum displays or art work that none of you have seen before, you have opportunities to learn together.

Remember, it is not necessary for the parent to have all the answers! There is always room to learn and grow, and you probably want your children to know that learning never ends. When you model learning for your children, it slightly shifts the hierarchy in your family structure. Suddenly, you the parent become a student. Shifts in power structure, even if only momentary, result in shifts in communication. A slight, momentary change in family roles may open communication doors you never expected and provide new opportunities for building common ground.

Volunteer, together!

Select a volunteer opportunity as a family unit. Consider "adopting" an elderly couple or a single person you know is lonely. Together, plan activities that will lift their spirits. Become a "personal shopping family" for a shut-in. Perhaps your church knows of someone who needs the help your family can offer.

You may prefer an activity less directly involved with other people. There is often a need for volunteers to help with a city project, such as improving a park or playground or beautifying a part of the city. Animal shelters need volunteers. There may be opportunities for volunteers at your local zoo.

Perhaps yours is a very busy family with limited time available for volunteering. Get physical! As a family enter a walk for a specific cause! Make it an annual event that all family members prepare for by building stamina with weekly (or daily) family walks! What would it be like for your family to stand side by side serving the meal at the annual Thanksgiving community dinner for the homeless? What if your family helped Habitat for Humanity build one house? Can you imagine how enriched your entire family would be by participating in such a project, even once a year?

Needs are so widespread, that opportunities to volunteer are virtually endless. Most cities have a volunteer clearinghouse or United Way. Call and ask about opportunities to serve others together as a family. Emphasize that you are looking for opportunities for the whole family, and avoid being pulled apart by thoughts of separate opportunities to volunteer. Your goal is to build common ground.

Create a family cookbook, together!

Diet issues aside! Food is undoubtedly the most powerful memory builder. It is well known that our sense of smell is the strongest sensory trigger of memories. Smells from the kitchen usually provide the fondest, loving memories we recall. Be sure those fond, loving memories are immortalized in a family cookbook your children can take with them on their own journey into parenthood.

This family activity may include extended family members, as you gather recipes of family favorites. It may involve visits to gather, even taste those recipes. The family photography buff might take pictures of family favorites to include in your recipe book. The family journalist might write special memories related to particular dishes to accompany the recipes. Let the artist or crafter in the family, design the cover and separating pages. Make copies of your cookbook for everyone in the family to enjoy for a lifetime.

Research a topic, together!

Sometimes it seems more difficult to know family members as intimately as we know our friends. One suggestion that may open doors to increased intimacy and understanding between family members is this: Listen!

In your daily comings and goings among family members, listen carefully for clues to areas of interest for each family member. When you hear a special interest, explore it further, as a family. Ask what different areas about that topic might be discovered, if some research were done. Over dinner discuss the topic and help each family member select a different area of that topic to research. Set a time limit—a week is usually good. At the end of that time, gather the family to share what they have learned in their research of the topic.

Listen for clues to how interested each family member has become with the topic. If there seems to be strong interest, continue researching that topic. If interest seems low, discuss other areas of interest they've noticed in each other. Then set research plans in motion on the new topic.

The topic is not as important as the activity. The issue is not whether your family gains public recognition for having the most knowledge, nor gaining the Nobel Peace Prize on the topic. The issue is simply to learn more about one another and to draw closer as a family. By sharing each other's interests you are building common ground.

A number of years ago I traveled to Oregon to spend the Christmas holiday with my oldest daughter. She was living with friends who graciously invited me to stay in their home. Tom, a widower of many years, was approximately seventy then and full of enthusiasm. He was an involved individual. He cared for his home, played with his dog, shopped, cooked, visited with friends, traveled and was always seeking interesting activities.

Tom had a special interest in words. Over the years he became well known among family and friends for his daily word activities. Each day he selected a new word to research and use, which he posted on the refrigerator for all to see. My first morning there, he posted the word, "viaduct."

He then researched his word, learning its origin and as many definitions and uses of the word as he could find. Of course, over the years he had acquired a virtual arsenal of word reference books. He established a goal for himself to use the word a certain number of times in normal conversation during the day.

As I was sitting at the kitchen table enjoying my first cup of coffee, Tom's nephew joined us. Almost before saying "good morning" he inquired, "Hey, Tom. What's our word for the day?"

As the day went on, virtually each person we met made the same inquiry. Then one asked, "Tom, how's the 'AMITOR project' going?"

Assuming that "AMITOR" was an acronym I was not familiar with, I asked, "What does AMITOR stand for?"

Tom explained: Years before, he began searching for an English word that meant the opposite of "predator," describing a "good person." He felt there were enough English words depicting hatred and "bad people." When he could not find the word he was seeking, he created a word, "amitor"—one who has reverence for life and remains nonviolent. He then set his sights on having "amitor" established as a legitimate word in the English dictionary.

Tom's family and friends traveled the journey with him. He created a slogan, adopting the giraffe, a most peaceful creature, as his logo, and began researching how to have a word placed in the dictionary. "Amitor" seemed to creep into most of his conversations, and Tom freely gave out trinkets he had imprinted with the "amitor" logo.

Although, sadly Tom recently passed away, his family continues his AMITOR project. I don't think the importance of the project lies in having a word added to the English language. I think the importance of the "Amitor Project" is the marvelous legacy of sharing, bonding and great fun Tom left to all who knew him—especially his family.

Perform Random Acts of Kindness, Together!

There are so many disenfranchised people in this world. As a family, get your heads together and decide on random acts of kindness you can do together to bring even one of these lost people "into the fold"—simple "just because" acts, that will provide a sense of belonging to those who are lost and alone. Perhaps there is someone you've noticed at your workplace who seems isolated, or even someone at your church who seems to be having difficulty becoming involved. Occasionally, those lost and lonely people are right there in your own family.

Just remember how "franchised" you feel when you receive a "just because card," a "just because gift" or "just because phone call or visit" out of nowhere!

In one of the darkest moments of my life, I received a "Hang In There" card from some people I hadn't seen or talked to in six years! The card arrived on one of my own darkest days. How could they have known how much I needed that encouragement? As I reflected on this puzzling concept, my spirit soared as I realized how "franchised" I was as a member of God's family! God knew I needed the card; God told them I needed the card, they merely responded with a simple random act of kindness that made all the difference in the world to me! I have a feeling their random act of kindness was a family project—they all signed the card! I have to wonder whether reaching out together as a family, made a difference in their lives; I know it did in mine!

Build traditions, together!

Establish unique, precious moments that become traditions in your family. Create your own family holiday or hold "Un-birthday Parties." On a day totally unrelated to a birthday, celebrate the **person,** as though it was their birthday! Hold "Family Entertainment" nights. You know how children like to sing and dance during dinner? When they are little we think, "It's so cute." One day it becomes "Not so cute anymore." Why is that? If a child, or any family member for that matter, expresses a talent, encourage the entertainment to continue. Once a month everyone prepares entertainment for the family. Include extended family, as well!

Remember the activities you enjoyed as a child and incorporate them into a monthly Family Fun Time. A tradition does not need to be elaborate. Instead of costly gifts for birthdays or holidays, make it a tradition to give time. I received this through the e-mail:

How Much Is Your Time Worth?

The man came home from work late again, tired and irritated, to find his five-year old son waiting for him at the door.

"Daddy, may I ask you a question?"

"Yes, sure, what is it?" replied the man.

"Daddy, how much money do you make an hour?"

"That's none of your business. What makes you ask such a thing?" the man said angrily.

"I just want to know. Please tell me how much do you make an hour," pleaded the little boy.

"If you must know, I make $20.00 an hour."

"Oh!" the little boy replied, head bowed. Looking up he said, "Daddy, may I borrow $10.00 please?"

The father was furious. "If the only reason you wanted to know how much money I make is just so you can borrow some to buy a silly toy or some other nonsense, then you march yourself straight to your room and go to bed. Think about why you're being so selfish. I work long, hard hours everyday and don't have time for such childish games."

The little boy quietly went to his room and shut the door. The man sat down and started to get even madder about the little boy's questioning. How dare he ask such questions only to get some money?

After an hour or so, the man had calmed down and started thinking he may have been a little hard on his son. Maybe there was something he really needed to buy with that $10.00 and he really didn't ask for money very often.

The man went to the door of the little boy's room and opened the door. "Are you asleep son?" he asked.

"No, Daddy, I'm awake," replied the boy.

"I've been thinking, maybe I was too hard on you earlier," said the man. It's been a long day and I took my aggravation out on you. Here's that $10.00 you asked for."

The little boy sat straight up, beaming. "Oh thank you, Daddy!" he yelled. Then he reached under his pillow and pulled out some more crumpled up bills. The man, seeing the boy already had money, started to get angry again. The little boy slowly counted out his money and then looked up at his father.

"Why did you want more money if you already had some?" the father grumbled.

"Because I didn't have enough, but now I do," the little boy replied. "Daddy, I have $20.00 now, can I buy an hour of your time?"

—Author Unknown

Worship together!

Most importantly, incorporate a regular, daily prayer time into your family's busy schedule. Attend worship services together, as a family.

And all thy children shall be taught of the Lord; and great shall be the peace of thy children."   — *Isaiah: 54:13*

Break Time

*Six days thou do thy work, and on the seventh day thou
shalt rest...* — *Exodus 23:12*

There is precious little time to communicate on any level at the
speed our society whirls. Seeking ever-evasive fulfillment, we
will whirl away until we ultimately offer ourselves as fodder
for "dust to dust." Somehow, I do not think self-implosion was the
original intent. The irony is, while we have negligible time for communication, when we assess the aftermath of broken relationships
and events-gone-wrong, we consistently find "lack of communication"
at its base. Yet, we keep whirling, finding less and less time for communication. It is a very vicious cycle we cannot seem to break. While
we spin out of control, we continuously seek ways to be in command
of our little corner of the world. That is not an easy task.

Society as a whole, is a system in which our family is but one
of a multitude of smaller systems. As individuals, we are virtually a
microcosmic piece of even that smaller family system. To comfortably function in the larger system, we rumple ourselves up to fit the
societal norms; in doing that we find ourselves whirling at more and
more dangerous speeds. If we desire a more peaceful conclusion to our
lives, we will find ways to slow down to a more manageable speed.

*Years ago I came to the realization that when there was not time
to slow down, and I desperately needed a break, I found a way to take
care of myself. I got sick! It is still perfectly legitimate in our society to
be sick. With nose running and glazed, feverish eyes, it is okay to take
a day off from the race. No one questions or criticizes. In fact, it some-*

times elicits a bit of sympathy. Getting sick did not exactly fit into the pleasurable lifestyle I was seeking, but it served its purpose—it gave me permission to slow down.

Now I have found a more effective way to slow down; I give myself permission.

Lorraine and I worked together in northeastern Colorado and left our jobs at about the same time. We had been utterly devoted to our jobs almost twenty hours a day, rarely taking a break. She recently reminded me that it wasn't enough that we put in sixteen hours a day at the office, but we went home and called each other to resolve unfinished business from the cozy comfort of our beds.

I moved back to Texas and a few months later when my house sold, I drove back to Colorado for the closing. I was eagerly looking forward to staying with Lorraine and her family. She had not taken another job and there would be time to visit and just enjoy one another, a luxury we had not afforded ourselves when we were working together.

For several days we spent the cool, crisp mornings together on her deck, leisurely drinking coffee, reminiscing and laughing. We spent our days together creating new memories by leisurely wandering shops or meandering through her gardens. In the evenings we leisurely sat together after dinner, catching up on more recent happenings.

As my visit was coming to an end, Lorraine invited mutual friends and former co-workers over to see me while I was in town. On the morning of the gathering I awoke to find Lorraine already whirling through the house, getting a head start on preparations for the evening get-together. I am not sure I said it aloud, but I did think, "This is it? We whirl through life in our jobs; we whirl through life in our homes. When does the whirling end? Oh," I thought, "when we die!"

I did not like the sound of that. Incessant whirling only the grave can stop. I called to Lorraine firmly, "Break Time!" Lorraine added, "You bet! We're semi-retired!" We sat together with our morning coffee, again laughing, remembering old times and making more new memories.

Somewhere we must have heard that rest is to be abhorred, as only for the lazy. Not wanting to appear lazy, we came to believe that we must always be "doing something" to be worthy contenders in the race of life. It now seems society as a whole has taken that notion to a new level. We have acquired a talent for looking productive by running at faster and faster speeds.

Not only do electronic devices help us run faster, they desensitize us, serving to numb us from the pain of ceaseless running, while simultaneously bombarding us with the means to run faster. Marketing texts tell us that to increase profits vendors must appeal to what the people want most—speed! "Our product will do it for you—faster." Ads tell us that the speed of the product will simplify our life and make us happier. In reality, these new speeding products only add new complications, increasing our frustrations with confusing messages telling us we are not yet running fast enough. Now we need a new product, something that will go even faster—fast is not fast enough. If we could just go faster, we would achieve the benefits promised!

For the family, this perpetual race generally means that communication diminishes, often eventually ceasing, as each individual whirls away in an orbit all his own. Parents, simply trying to keep a roof over the family, clothes on their backs and food on the table, must speed away in different directions to forage for resources. Children are left on their own to figure out which road they will speed down. Sometimes, left to their own devices, they make very poor choices of the roads they take.

As role models, parents serve as mirrors reflecting to their children the manner in which they are expected to behave. When children observe their parent-mirror reflecting speed, they speed. Unfortunately they rarely have the opportunity to see where their parents are speeding. So, they hypothesize when they set off on their own race. In making up their own route, they often race down perilous roads.

When, as parents, we occasionally reach plateaus where we can rest for a moment, we look for our children and they are gone. They became weary of waiting for us to provide their boundaries, soothe their wounds or offer the touches of affection and signs of approval they were seeking. They have raced off elsewhere to fill those needs. With no one to share our momentary resting stop, we get back in the race. However, this race has no end. There is no goal line. We don't know how to stop!

What we really need is a product to slow us down.

Like a perpetual motion machine, the whirling does not cease, unless we make it cease. Someone must take the bull by the horns and say, "Break Time!" Who will be the one to say "Break Time!" in your family? Who will add, "You bet"?

Communication is the primary key to every relationship. Whether verbal or non-verbal, we communicate to connect and stay connected with others. Notice that it is very difficult to communicate when you are racing at high rates of speed. Therefore, if communication is key to building relationships and we are racing too fast to communicate, there will be no relationships—or at best, only superficial relationships.

Superficial relationships work well, if we wish to avoid intimacy. However, children yearn for, and fervently seek, intimacy with their parents from the time they are born. When they do not receive the intimacy they crave from their parents, they will continue to seek until they find it somewhere else. Unfortunately, having no role model for intimacy, they often engage in harmful, even abusive relationships, in what becomes a futile effort to find a warm, intimate relationship. Nothing can replace the intimacy a child desires from a parent. Efforts at substitution are therefore fruitless. The resulting frustration sets the child up for potential failure in future relationships.

For this reason alone, it is critical that parents regularly "take a break" to periodically assess whether they are operating at safe rates of speed, or at speeds too fast for their children to catch up with them. If you assess that your speed is out of control, or even slightly detrimental to your relationship with your child, you may want to alter how fast you are willing to race outside of the family, and call loudly for "Break Time."

Racing To Nowhere

The labour of the foolish wearieth every one of them, because he knoweth not how to go to the city.
— *Ecclesiastes 10:15*

When I was a teen, my mother asked me what I wanted out of life. My profound response was, "I just plan to have fun." She was appalled. "Life is not about 'fun'. It's about work, hard work, and, you'd better get started!"

Unfortunately, she turned on her heel and raced off to somewhere without providing me with any suggestions for how to "get started." So, I set out alone on the "Happy Go Lucky Road to Fun."

Along the road to "Fun," I found unexpected detours to places that were not much fun. The first major detour was divorce. My understanding of marriage, from the mirror I learned from, was "never fight in front of the children and life will be swell." My parents prided themselves in never arguing in front of my sister or me. They were proficient at never letting us know there was a problem in the world. This certainly reinforced my situation-comedy role models. The strange thing was that while we looked really good on the outside—nice house, nice cars, nice clothes, private schools, and country club—it just felt terrible on the inside.

My husband's father died when he was ten. His mother, quite unusual for her time, set her sights on a career and became a bookkeeper. She had little time for parenthood. Her children seemed to raise themselves.

Thus, neither of us had a full picture of what marriage really entailed. We apparently assumed marriage just "happened." Our arguments signaled to me that something was wrong. My parent-mirror had no arguments. When children came and arguments burst forth in front of them, it was clear to me that something was seriously wrong. My model clearly indicated that children never heard parents argue. Obviously, I was in the wrong marriage. There were four children by the time I reached that conclusion.

The next detour was single parenting. I had no mirror at all for that. My parenting mirror model stayed together, and will for the duration. They are eighty-four now and can probably count on one hand the number of days they've spent apart. Of course, my mother informed me that I had done the wrong thing, getting divorced. I wondered if she weren't right, because single parenting was certainly not "Fun"!

So, I sought "Fun" down the career path. While I truly found satisfaction in my work, I found more unpleasant detours that no one had prepared me for. I thought that if you worked hard, were a loyal employee and achieved productive results, there would be appreciation. I found that to not necessarily be so. I thought you "did what was right" and rewards would be forthcoming. I found that absolutely not to be so. In fact, when I found and reported what I believed to be unscrupulous, even abusive practices, my efforts were met with anger, even rage. That part never was much "Fun."

Then one day I faced a huge, most unpleasant and unexpected detour. Almost two years after the divorce, my former husband filed for custody of our children. It was many years before I learned his purported reason for this sudden decision to file for custody. He had come to pick up the children and I was sick in bed. In fact, I had been sick all week and actually called him to help me with the kids. The house was a terrible mess. He said later that he determined at that moment he would "not allow his children to be raised in a pig pen." The fact that I had contracted hepatitis and landed in the hospital for a week was no deterrent; the court hearings proceeded.

The school principal, my children's teachers, our baby-sitter, neighbors and friends all testified that I was an involved, caring and loving mother. He had but one witness. To avoid clouding the issue, I will only say that this one witness was "a man of the cloth." Small world that we live in, I had roomed with his daughter in college. I don't think he even knew that, in fact, he barely knew me at all. I don't recall that we exchanged any more than a "hello" in the years we attended his place of worship. What could he offer that would make a difference? My former husband's attorney asked him several questions, but I only recall one response; "She has sinned and cannot be redeemed." And, what was that sin? "She married a man who is not of her religion," he told the jury.

When the jury declared the children should live with their father, I was aghast. My attorney was astonished as well. Two of the jurors came up to us in the hallway afterward. They wanted me to know that they had not voted with the rest of the jury. One of them said, that while she did not know me, she also was faced with a "small world experience" in the courtroom, when one of my witnesses turned out to be someone she knew well. It was my children's school principal. She said, "That is a person who tells it like it is. If you weren't a good mother, she would not have wasted a minute letting us know." She added, "The rest of the jury really was swayed by the [clergy]."

I dug in my heels and worked harder, played harder and raced down the highway 150 miles one way, each and every weekend, retrieving my children and bringing them home. Six hundred miles I drove every weekend, to spend a few hours with my children. This was definitely not the road to "Fun;" in fact, that detour took me as far away from "Fun" as I could get. I wanted to get off this road to "Fun," but how could I accomplish that?

When we are racing down a road to destruction, we do not take time to notice where the road is leading, until we are forced to face the consequences. In addiction counseling we would call that "hitting bottom." Everyone's "bottom" is different. Would you not think being separated from one's children would be the greatest "bottom" anyone could hit? Not necessarily! In my case the road was paved with more blame, anger, even rage, none of which seemed to be getting me on the road to "Fun." It would be awhile before I came to my personal "bottom."

When you are in the Parenting Business, your children are likely to follow you on the roads you choose. Children even follow us to our "bottom," sometimes surpassing us to reach their own. If we can force ourselves to slow down the pace, or even screech to a halt, we might be able to gain a new perspective and begin operating at a less dangerous speed. Then, perhaps the connections between parent and child will have the time needed for opportunities to strengthen and grow.

Fragile! Do Not Break!

Train up a child in the way he should go; and when he is
old, he will not depart from it. — *Proverbs 22:6*

It is never too late to turn around and head in the other direction. If we allow ourselves to learn from our mistakes, it is not important where we have been. Where we go from here, is what truly matters. In the Parenting Business, experience provides needed wisdom—inversely. Would it not be best to have 20/20 hindsight, **before** venturing down the actual parenting highway? That will never happen. The best we can do is to learn from others' 20/20 hindsight, and seek parenting skills that work for us.

I realized that I was ill equipped for the parenting job I'd undertaken the moment the nurse thrust that pink bundle at me. My first reaction was, "Where are the instructions?" My second was, "Fragile! Do Not Break!"

Too late! I was on the parenting highway for the duration.

While I scrambled to gather tools for parenting, after the fact, my own children suffered several serious bumps and bruises. Along the parenting road I found several jars of ointment to add to my parenting toolbox. They relieved some stinging pains. Thankfully, children are resilient; however some scars remain for a lifetime and require additional applications of ointment throughout the years. As parents, I believe it is our responsibility to continuously seek new tools for healing old wounds and for new hazards that will cause new bruises, because the Parenting Business does not end until we end. Our children need us, indefinitely.

Despite all the jostling my own children received, they fortunately remained sufficiently resilient to respond when I found my bottom and began to change directions in parenting. When the doctor announced "cancer," I finally hit my "bottom," which jolted me into the reality that I was headed in absolutely the wrong direction. The good thing about hitting bottom is that it forces us to look up for the answers. In looking up, way up to God, I found a new way of life that has been a lot more fun than the roads I initially thought would lead me there. Fortunately, my children remained sufficiently intact to respond when I found a much better road to "Fun." I am so thankful for that, because just as my children were beginning their own independent lives as young adults, I began a new route in the Parenting Business. It was then that I learned how really fragile these precious gifts from God actually can be.

When I entered the professional arena, the only family I knew with significant familiarity was ours. I only knew from our experiences what worked and what did not. Today, having had the opportunity to work with many families over the years, I have a comparison. I now know that children really can break.

Mental Sabotage Breaks Children

Fathers, provoke not your children to anger, lest they be discouraged.   *— Colossians 3:21*

Initially, Jimmy's parents seemed headed down a reasonably straight road. Childhood sweethearts each worked in a traditional, respectable, well-paying job. Both were from intact families, serving to model some stability for them. A couple of years after marrying, a baby boy was born. He would be their only child.

When Jimmy was two, his parents bought their first home located far off the main road outside a small, quiet, rural community. They planned to spend their free time fixing up the run-down house and sprucing up the grounds. I saw the house, and know their plans were never realized. Instead, Jimmy's parents used their isolated house to manufacture drugs and hold illegal gamecock fights. We will never know their side of the story, because Jimmy's parents are dead. He killed them both when he was twelve. His grandmother was the only available family member to shed light on Jimmy's tales of horror.

She recalled feeling very uncomfortable when she went to visit her son and his family. "He wasn't treated like a child," she told me one day during a rare visit to the juvenile facility.

"How do you mean?" I questioned.

"When he was just a little thing—maybe three or four, we were visiting outside in the yard and his mother sent him inside to make iced tea for us."

"You mean, get the tea?"

"No mam!" the grandmother stated. "She sent him in to boil water, dunk tea bags and get that tea outside for us."

"What else made you uncomfortable?" I asked.

"The way they talked to him. They ordered him around demanding he fetch things for them—do things for them. It was like he was their slave."

"This was all when he was three or four?" I asked.

"Yes. I never saw him after that, until this thing happened. So, I know he had to be no more than four."

"Why is it you never saw him after that?"

Jimmy's grandmother reported, "My son barred me from their property."

She explained that her husband, Jimmy's grandfather had been ill for years, and it was his wish to die in his own home. She granted his wish, bringing him home from the nursing facility, and he died shortly thereafter. She said her son twisted this, saying that her decision to move his father out of the nursing home had killed him. Her son refused to speak to her, and she never saw him again until his own funeral.

Jimmy's version was more graphic and involved eight more years of torment.

Jimmy remembered when he was six, his father was building what "looked like a tree house, but was really a lookout post."

"A lookout post for what?" I asked.

"A lookout post for the law," Jimmy stated.

"What was that for?"

"I was supposed to stay up there with a walkie-talkie when they had cock fights, and call him if I saw the law coming down the road."

How did Jimmy's father control his young child, to assure his illicit dealings were not revealed? He abused Jimmy mentally, as much as physically. For example, he demanded that Jimmy, age six, haul lumber up a ten-foot ladder to help him build that tree-house-lookout. To show Jimmy who was boss, he grabbed a piece of lumber from Jimmy's hands and used it to push over the ladder, knocking Jimmy some ten feet to the ground into a barbed wire fence. The fall left Jimmy with deep scars in his arms and body, and knocked out one of his front teeth.

His parents loaded him into their truck and took him to the dentist. On the way, Jimmy's father pinched his leg, hard, while he drilled into Jimmy the routine for the dentist's office. At the dentist, while both parents looked on refusing to leave Jimmy's side, Jimmy dutifully reported how his mouth hit the handlebars when he fell off his bike into a pile of gravel.

Jimmy's father probably controlled his wife in the same manner. Jimmy recalled that his mother had found a stray dog that she raised and loved. One day the dog had puppies. He and his mother were playing with the new puppies, when Jimmy's father came over and told Jimmy to go get a pillowcase. Dutifully, Jimmy went into the house and came back with the pillowcase. By then, his father had gathered some bricks.

He told Jimmy to put the bricks inside the pillowcase. Jimmy did. Then his father told him to put the puppies into the pillowcase with the bricks. After Jimmy had done his father's bidding, his father told him to slam the pillowcase into the ground and kill all of the puppies. His mother looked on sobbing, but did nothing to stop the incident. When Jimmy stopped, his father dumped the contents of the pillowcase on the ground. One of the puppies survived. His father picked up a brick himself, and smashed the last living puppy before Jimmy's eyes.

That kind of mental torture is typical in domestic violence cases. In this case, Jimmy's father controlled two people with his mental cruelty. If they did not comply, they could become like one of those puppies, they felt just as helpless.

The list of torture went on, involving yet another broken tooth. Ultimately Jimmy had two false front teeth by the age of twelve, yet no one was the wiser.

Did Jimmy ever tell? He says he told teachers and parents of friends, but no one believed him, because his parents were well respected in their small community. No one knew what went on in their isolated rural house. So, he gave up and stopped telling, as the abuse grew worse.

When Jimmy brought home a poor report card, he knew his father

*would beat him. He was not to do anything that would draw attention
to their family, and failing grades would require involvement with the
school. His mother was in the kitchen preparing dinner and his father was outside, when Jimmy went into their bedroom and grabbed
the shotgun. He took the gun into his own bedroom. When his father
came down the hall calling "Time to eat," Jimmy opened the door and
followed his father a few short steps and began firing. His father fell
dead at his feet.*

*Jimmy stepped over his father's body and proceeded to the kitchen
where his mother was putting dinner on the table. He raised the shotgun and pulled the trigger. She only had time to shout, "What are you
doing?" before she too lay dead at Jimmy's feet.*

*Jimmy packed up the family car, taking items important to a twelve-
year old boy—the portable television, some video games, tapes and some
clothes. He drove into town and stopped at a friend's, asking if he could
spend the night. Something about a twelve year old driving the family
car triggered suspicion. The friend's mother called the police.*

"Why didn't you just keep telling people, Jimmy?" I asked.

*"No one was going to stop him. He had lots of friends. They'd never
believe me—a snot-faced kid. I had to be the one to stop him."*

"But, why your mother?"

*"She was just as bad. She sat there and watched him do it to me.
She didn't even try to stop him."*

While the extreme nature of this case may not seem relevant to
your parenting, there are a number of reasons I share it here. We all
want to feel "in control." If we cannot feel in control outside of our
home, we will do all we can to gain control within our own domain.
While we may do that in much more subtle ways than Jimmy's parents,
we must be careful of how our efforts to control affect those around us.

It would seem in a parenting book there would be a step-by-step
process, defining how to raise a child. Unfortunately, people are not
mechanical and therefore cannot be programmed to respond to step-
by-step expectations. Therefore, we might look at what others have
done, rightly or wrongly, to make decisions about the parenting road
we will take. By looking at the extremes, we may find degrees of behavior in ourselves that if not checked, may well become damaging
to our own children.

In Jimmy's family, for whatever reasons, his father wanted total control over the family. He used mental conditioning—mind games, which he enhanced with physical abuse. We all play mind games to some extent to control various situations. Whenever we do not ask directly for what we want, but manipulate to meet our needs, we are playing a mind game. My mother played an interesting mind game she likely learned from her mother, who probably learned it from her mother, and so on.

About fifteen years ago, my sister and I were having a phone conversation. My sister suggested I do something. I do not even remember the topic now, because the insight I gained after a lifetime of wondering erased that part of the conversation.

I responded in earnest, "But you should do that. Mother always says you're much better at that than I am."

I could almost hear how stunned my sister was, when she retorted, "That's not true. She always says you do that better than me..."

The light suddenly dawned for both of us, simultaneously, as we continued to compare notes. Not once was either of us told that we did well on our own merits, however numerous times we were told how well the other had done.

Was it an innocent comment? No. As a comment repeated numerous times, it was likely intentionally intended to inspire each of us to achieve more, work harder, be "more successful." Instead, unbeknownst to either of us, it established an ever-widening wedge between my sister and me; it gave me an intense distaste for competition; it drove my sister to move as far away as possible, without leaving the country, and unfortunately, our relationship has always remained tenuous. I attribute a great deal of that to the well-intentioned effort of our mother to control, by manipulating her children into becoming the kind of people she wanted us to be.

Granted, mind games were something she learned from her parenting role model. However, although long ago forgiven, I believe that as the parent, it was her responsibility to assess how well that behavior served her own family. She did not make that assessment. Had she but looked around, she would have noted that her mother's five daughters had all moved to live equilaterally spaced throughout the country, having very little to do with one another. The pattern had been passed from generation to generation. No one stopped it, until the day my sister and I inadvertently compared notes!

Mind games backfire. In our family, mind games divided the family geographically. In Jimmy's case, mind games divided a family permanently.

Emotional Remote Control Breaks Children

Keep thy heart with all diligence; for out of it are the issues of life.   *— Proverbs 4:23*

Jared was one of the most unlikely candidates for a juvenile offenders setting. The youngest of three children, Jared was a slightly overweight, fresh-faced kid of fourteen. He was a bright student, intellectually more mature than his years. He was involved in community activities, especially as a scout. His father, a professional, had been a scout leader for years. His mother was a full time homemaker. Jared and his family were very active in their church. From all outward appearances, this was an upstanding child from an upstanding family.

Then one day, Jared learned a girl he had a crush on was babysitting at the house across the street. After dinner, he quietly left his house, walked across the street and into his neighbor's open garage, where he retrieved several hunting knives he knew were there. He walked into the house through the garage and stood patiently waiting for the young girl to finish a phone conversation with her boyfriend.

When she hung up the phone, Jared immediately began stabbing her. The stab wounds were so numerous, the doctors lost count at one hundred and thirty five entry points—thirty-nine of which they found in her hands. She tried desperately to defend herself.

Jared's rage was so great, that when knives broke off in her body, he returned to the garage where he retrieved more knives, and continued his rage-filled assault until he was satisfied that she was dead. Saturated in the young girl's blood, Jared walked back across the street, into his house and went straight to his mother and told her what he had done.

When I first met Jared's mother, without questioning she volunteered, "I don't understand his sentence. She didn't die. She's flitting around town like nothing happened." Jared's father was silent.

As Jared worked through his rage, we invited his parents to participate in weekly counseling sessions. Jared's mother repeatedly interrupted any dialogue that appeared vaguely related to her feelings. She sidetracked incessantly, veering onto topics that were light and carefree and in no way related to her, their family or Jared's offense.

Finally, Jared himself worked up the courage to tell her directly and specifically that he needed her to hear what he had to say. We thought she finally heard his need to connect with her on an emotional level. Unfortunately, when it was suggested that she had been so preoccupied with repressing her own unresolved emotional issues that she had been unable to respond to Jared's emotional needs, she abruptly stopped the session, saying, "I will never talk about those things. What happened in my family is my business."

Jared's mother left the counseling room and refused to return despite my urging and Jared's. Ultimately, in counseling we worked on Jared letting go of his rage toward his mother. In fact, his attempt to kill the young girl was really his attempt to kill his mother. This innocent young girl had unknowingly repeated Jared's mother's behavior. She refused to engage in an emotional connection with Jared, and he cared deeply for her. He longed for his mother to emotionally connect with him, and she refused. He felt invisible when, blood-soaked from his offense, he specifically sought out his mother, subconsciously thinking that this might finally gain the emotional connection with her that he so craved. If he could just make her respond to him! Sadly, it was not to happen. His mother was so intensely hanging on to her own childhood pain, that she had no emotional strength to make room for an emotional connection with Jared.

If you are preoccupied with your own issues that absolutely does not mean your child will slaughter a neighbor. It may mean, however, that you are missing a wonderful relationship with a child who will seek attention elsewhere, by some other means.

It is critical that we resolve our own emotional pain, to be capable of connecting emotionally with our children. When our own unresolved issues are too painful for us to deal with, we do not have the emotional energy to embrace any further discomfort others might send our way, even our own child. When our child experiences a difficulty even vaguely resembling our own repressed and buried pain, we shut down. We are not emotionally accessible. We shut out our own child. It is not a malicious act; it is a self-protective act. It is also an immeasurably harmful act.

Ripping Into Pieces Breaks Children

*No servant can serve two masters: for either he will hate
the one and love the other; or else he will hold to the one,
and despise the other...*   *— Luke 16:13*

It would be so much easier to believe that if we could just "fix"
our child, without fixing ourselves, all would be well. Unfortunately,
I can give clear 20/20 hindsight testimony to the fact that when the
problem is in the family; "fixing the child" only comes from "fixing
the parent."

*One Friday evening as I was racing the 150 miles down the highway
to retrieve my children, that "still small voice within" said, "You know,
this disrupts **their** lives at least as much as it disrupts yours." I had a
couple of hours to ponder that thought before they, less than eagerly,
piled into the car for the 150-mile trip back to my house.*

*We puttered around the house, ate meals at home and pretended
to be a "normal" family. I did not want them to come to the conclusion that weekends with Mommy would be sprinkled with Disneyland
glitz, but wanted them to believe that we were still a family. As Sunday
drew to a close and it was nearing time to return them to their father,
I suddenly felt sick. I spent the last hour in bed. It took me a long time
to realize that I did this **every** Sunday. It was my way of dealing with
my depression over their leaving.*

*On the way back home after returning the children to their father,
I thought more about the disruption of our lives. In fact, the children
could not really build friendships or engage in weekend activities with
schoolmates and neighbors, because they were traveling down the highway to visit me. In fact, they could not establish a life anywhere. They
were being pulled from one home to another having no opportunity
to establish roots in either place. I decided to let them have a life and
quit tearing them apart. Soon after that weekend, I announced I would
only pick them up twice a month.*

*Probably because it was such a painful decision and such a pain-
ful time in my life, I do not remember exactly how the ensuing events
unfolded. However, within a year of the custody fiasco, their father had
decided our oldest daughter needed to live with me. Next he decided
our youngest daughter needed to live with me. Within two years he*

had also decided our oldest son was impossible for him to handle, and he angrily returned him to me. I did not care how they came back. I was happy to have them with me.

At some point along that road, both their father and I grew up. I truly do not remember who initiated "growing up," but we began meeting halfway to exchange the children, making the trip half as long. At some point we decided to actually sit down and have a soda at the time of the exchange! At some point we also decided how child support issues would be handled, without an attorney. At some point we actually reached peace between us. The day I realized I had no anger, no hatred, no animosity toward the children's father, was truly a day of freedom. Although I did not recognize it at the time, it was also the day I began having more energy to devote to parenting my children.

A number of years ago their father and I had a very special opportunity to actively be parents—jointly—to our children. Then, I think we both knew we had reached true peace. We both had the honor of walking our first child, Kayla, down the aisle, together giving her hand in marriage. Since that time, the opportunities to jointly parent our children seem to have inexplicably increased, almost exponentially. It is almost as though we are pasting our children back together, after all too long tearing them apart. The peace we have experienced from totally letting go of the past is truly a blessing.

It might have ended very differently.

Almost ten years ago now, our granddaughter was dedicated at a wonderful ceremony at her maternal great-grandparent's church, high in the beautiful, rugged Texas hill country. Following the services, we all went to their nearby home for barbecue and an afternoon together. Then it was time to once again go our separate ways.

As we arranged carpools back to town, Kayla and I offered to drive her youngest brother, Joshua. As we headed off in the dark through the winding hill country roads, the conversation turned to their younger days. It suddenly became very quiet as Kayla and I realized that Joshua was silently crying in the back seat. We too became tearful, remembering days that were not so pleasant as this one.

When Joshua finally was able to speak, with a great deal of obvious pain, he intensely directed his words at me. "Why wouldn't you all let me be with my brother and sisters? What was wrong with me that you wouldn't let me be with them?"

Neither Kayla nor I understood what he was saying. In fact, his statement stunned us. No one ever denied him his brother and sisters; in fact, that thought had never even entered anyone's mind. Ironically, he was the one child everyone saw as "well put together"—there was "nothing wrong with him"!

*Joshua then recalled for us all those weekend visits. Their father and I thought we were doing something oh so noble, meeting midway, sharing time for a coke, **exchanging** children. What we hadn't realized was that in the exchange Joshua was rarely ever in the same home with his brother and sisters. Now a college junior, he still agonized wondering why his father and I had not allowed him to spend time with his brother and sisters.*

We all sobbed for the full hour trip back to the city, with me apologizing for our error and attempting to explain our thinking. We were all still in tears when we hit the lighted expressway of the city. Joshua was still so teary-eyed; he couldn't see to tell us where to exit! We stopped in a parking lot and continued our tearful encounter. The night fortunately ended in hugs and tearful, but loving good-byes. Gratefully, we had the opportunity for more healing. It could have been so very different.

Even when we think we are doing the right thing, we may be causing damage. That is why communication is so important. I have no idea why we never realized the damage we were doing to Joshua, while we thought we were being such models for visitation. We will never know the answer to that. We never asked the questions; in fact, we never made ourselves aware.

It serves no purpose now, rehashing who did what. We cannot undo a wrongdoing made well over twenty years ago. We can only pick up the pieces from here and move forward with that 20/20 hindsight, to avoid such mistakes in the future.

When we pull our children from pillar to post, we must realize they are experiencing serious pain. Even when we stop tearing them to pieces, we must make ourselves aware that scars remain. When, as adults now, my children opt to go to their father's for a holiday, it is my responsibility to deal with my feelings about that. It is my responsibility to assure that they do not become torn apart by guilt; sometimes that's tricky. While it is my responsibility to assure they do not feel they must divide their loyalties, at the same time I need to let them know I love them and wish we could be together. How can you do that without dividing loyalties?

We are both their parents. No matter what occurred between us, no matter whether we resolved our differences or not, as the leaders of our family we are the ones who will determine how well the children survive the mistakes we made. We are the ones who will determine whether they are ripped to pieces, or not. It takes something of a Solomon-like wisdom to stop tearing when our hearts are broken and our needs are unfulfilled. We must focus unselfishly on our children's hearts and needs. What is important is that they have the freedom to experience the love of both their parents.

Delicate Handling Breaks Children

> *Be strong and of good courage, fear not, nor be afraid of them; for the Lord thy God, He it is that doth go with thee; He will not fail thee, nor forsake thee.*
>
> — *Deuteronomy 31:6*

Brian is another child who seemed so unlike the stereotypical juvenile offender. An exceptionally good student, Brian was personable, attractive, athletic and gifted. He was in fact, at least on the surface, all of those things a parent would hope for in a child. He was polite, articulate—for a thirteen year old, humorous, talented, an all around pleasant, bright and cooperative child.

Brian was an only child, and his parents doted on him. Until he was ten, Brian was raised in a predominantly black neighborhood in a large city. He attended a predominantly black school and excelled in all that he undertook. He attended church regularly with his mother. Both of his parents held responsible, well-respected jobs, affording their family a comfortable lifestyle.

One morning when Brian was ten, he awoke to find a moving truck in front of the house and his parents packing. They told him then, with obvious excitement, that they were moving to a new home. He joined in helping them pack the truck. He never questioned their decision to move to their new home in an affluent, virtually all white suburb on the opposite side of town.

The move to their new home went uneventfully. The house was beautiful and spacious and in a lovely neighborhood. His parents were very happy with their new home.

Brian started school and was one of a handful of black youth attending; three were boys. According to Brian, when he entered middle school two years after the move, the coach recruited all three of the boys for the football team—without tryouts, saying, "You guys are always good at football. You don't need to try out." Brian's parents were so happy for him to be on the team, that he did not want to upset them, so mentioned nothing about the racial comment from the coach. Instead, he worked hard to excel in school and on the football team as well. His parents were proud of their new home and so pleased Brian was excelling in his new environment, that Brian never mentioned other racial comments he experienced.

The worst thing Brian recalled getting in trouble for, was once taking food into the den. Knowing he was not supposed to have food in the den, when he heard his parents coming he quickly slid the plate under the couch. His mother found it several days later, when she traced a trail of ants that suddenly appeared in the new house.

He had few bad memories, but did recall that when he was very young, perhaps five, he walked into his parents' bedroom where his father was seated on the end of the bed. He remembered a hose being pulled through the window and thrown over the door, and his mother begging his father not to kill himself. He thought his father planned to hang himself with the hose.

In fact, when we met with his parents and addressed this memory, Brian's father stated that Brian recalled the memory correctly, but he was actually sitting on the bed with a gun in his hand. In the way a young child integrates memories, the hose incident was totally separate and had something to do with trying to clean out air ducts. But, neither incident was ever discussed with Brian.

As for not including Brian in the plans to move from one neighborhood to another, his parents noted that they wanted a "better" life for their son, so they made the decision to move to a "better" neighborhood. They never thought this was a decision that required Brian's involvement; he was after all, just a child. They just assumed he would appreciate and enjoy it as much as they did.

One morning, when they had been in their new home just over two years, Brian and the neighbor girl were shooting baskets in the hoop between their houses. Suddenly the little girl, also twelve years old, told Brian she heard her phone ringing and ran into her house. Brian went inside his house as well, thinking, "I didn't hear any phone. I'm going *to call her in a minute and if she's not on the phone, I'm going to do something to her." As he was thinking, he was already preparing by removing a large kitchen knife from the drawer and placing it behind a vase in the front hallway. He called. She was not on the phone. When she answered, he told her he had something to show her.*

Brian watched as she ran past his living room window to his front door. He let her in and told her to go to the den. As she passed in front of him, he began stabbing her and continued to savagely torment and stab her with the kitchen knife until she was dead. He dragged her body to his backyard and hid it under a woodpile. He then attempted to clean up the blood in the hallway.

When his parents returned home and saw the blood still on the carpet, Brian told them he had a nosebleed. Although he'd had no previous nosebleeds, they asked no further questions, but put him to bed and hovered over him, lest the nosebleed return. When the girl's mother frantically came over to inquire whether Brian had seen her daughter, he told her, "No." The following day while mowing the yard, Brian's father found the girl's body.

Here were parents who did everything they believed to be in the best interest of their child. However, they failed to incorporate him into their hopes and dreams and problems. In a way, Brian's story reminds me very much of my own—never exhibit one problem in front of the children and if one should appear, brush it quickly under the carpet, eliminating all opportunities for your child to learn healthy problem solving skills.

If parents do not demonstrate how to appropriately resolve a problem, how will the child learn to solve his own problems? I believe that one enormous reason children physically demonstrate their anger and rage is that they have never learned to verbally express their feelings—especially their troubled feelings. They may have never seen a successful verbal resolution to a disagreement. When we protect our children from real emotions and real problems we are doing them a tremendous disservice.

It is interesting to note, that as delicately as Brian's parents treated him, he treated them equally as delicately. Their failure to share problems, concerns, even hopes and dreams with him, lead him to believe this was how people you love treat each other. Thus, when he had his own problems, he elected not to bother his parents with them, either. He chose instead, to handle the problem with the only tool he knew assuredly would resolve it, at the time.

When you sweep problems under the carpet, unless an army of ants appears to gnaw away at the growing mass, the pile builds and builds until it finally erupts. There is just not enough carpet to cover the growing tumor, and ultimately, it will expose itself. Fortunately, camouflaged problems are not always exposed in rage-filled violence. However, buried rage will eventually erupt.

Sometimes the rage turns inward, exposed as suicide or often other self-destructive behaviors, such as rage—substance abuse, abusive relationships, even self-mutilation. Often repressed rage is expressed through passive-aggressive behaviors, undermining one's own efforts or the efforts of others to achieve a successful relationship. Relationships are thwarted, pushed away with searing sarcasm, often disguised as an effort at humor. Success remains elusive in this innocent appearing game of self-sabotage.

No Handling At All Breaks Children

For the turning away of the simple shall slay them, and the prosperity of fools shall destroy them. — Proverbs 1:32

We attempt to relieve our rage any way we can, and it does not require a physical assault to express rage. Even materialism can be an expression of rage. It says, "If I can't physically take out my rage on you, I will still show you. I will have more, and bigger and better things than you ever thought of accumulating." The possessions actually become weapons. How do possessions become weapons?

Possessions become weapons when they interfere with relationships.

Children are not seeking "things." Material goods only become important to children when they are taught that material goods are important, sometimes even more important than **they** are to their parents. Children only want emotional connections with their parents. They want attention and approval; they want affection and acceptance, in its human form, not in material goods.

Have you ever noticed that after a birthday party or after unwrapping Christmas gifts, young children happily engage in activities with the boxes and wrapping paper and ribbons rather than the meticulously

selected gifts that were ever so carefully wrapped in those boxes and
ribbons? Children's material needs are very simple, until we teach
them to want more—until we teach them that possessions indicate
their worth. In some cases we even teach them that possessions are
worth more than they are.

I so appreciate the Bible verse that tells us, *"Lay not up for yourselves treasures upon earth, where moth and rust doth corrupt, and
where thieves break through and steal. But lay up for yourselves treasures in heaven, where neither moth nor rust doth corrupt and thieves
do not break through nor steal." — Matthew 6:19-20.* That verse is so
affirming for me—for all I thought and believed from the time I was
a child. Although I believed it, our family never lived it.

*My parents' house became a virtual mausoleum for earthly trea-
sures. When my children and I attempted to clean out years of accumulation several years ago, we found broken, decayed and rotted
possessions benefiting no one and no longer of any value. The garbage
pile grew deeper and deeper as we disposed of these useless amassed
possessions. It reminded me that when my mother's twin sister died,
my cousin told me, "Thirty years of Denver telephone books I had to
throw away—thirty years of phone books! What was that for?" My
mother would say, "You never know what might have value." I would
say, "Didn't her daughter have value? Didn't I have value? When did
we get buried beneath this worthless accumulation of possessions?"*

It is impossible for a child to compete for a parent's attention when
the competition is in the form of inanimate objects. Becoming en-
amored with inanimate objects happens so subtly that the consumer-
parent is virtually unaware of the shift in priorities from children, to
things. The child may yell and scream for attention, certainly acting
out in ways that receive negative attention—for any attention is better than no attention at all. Or, there is an alternative.

*Darren was from an upper middle class family. Their home in
the suburbs of a large city was well appointed. The family drove fine
cars. The boat was used for entertaining his father's business associ-
ates. While the family plane was used for business trips, it was also
the vehicle that took the family and their friends on trips to exciting,
glamorous vacation spots. In all, the family had most of the luxuries
money could buy.*

Years before, Darren's older brother became involved with drugs and his family spent tens of thousands of dollars placing him in exclusive residential treatment programs, yet he remained an active drug abuser. Darren determined that he would make up for the problems he perceived his brother caused his parents. He became an over-achiever. A very popular youth, he was quarterback of the high school football team and excelled in school. With all the material possessions any youth could possibly want, he appeared to be well on his way to a most successful future, until the afternoon he took his father's rifle and shot both of his parents.

With all those material possessions at his disposal, Darren never acquired the only possessions he truly wanted—his parents' attention, acceptance, approval and affection. They were so busy acquiring possessions and using possessions to impress outsiders, they failed to notice Darren's super-human efforts to excel in every way possible. They failed to take time to attend his football games. They failed to cheer his straight "A" report cards. They failed to notice anything about him on any level. It was almost as though he did not exist. Although praise and recognition came from many others, it never came from the only ones that truly mattered to him—his parents. Then one day, one critical comment from his father caused the resentment to erupt into overflowing rage, and he went from an upstanding super-human, over-achiever to a cold-blooded murderer. At a time like that material possessions mean nothing.

Self-absorption in any form can easily become an addiction. When a parent is self-absorbed with any addiction, he appears to be present, yet is unreachable—emotionally unavailable. It is almost better for the parent to be physically absent. When a child is physically abandoned, at least he can make up self-protective tales of how the parent was kidnapped by a band of pirates, an alien spaceship or lost at sea—self-protective tales that permit the child to believe he is accepted, approved of and loved. When parents are physically present, but emotionally absent, whether they intend to send the message or not, there is no way for the child to avoid the perception that he is just not important to them. Emotional abandonment breaks children.

Connecting

Salt is good, but if the salt have lost his saltiness, where-with will ye season it? Have salt in yourselves, and have peace one with another.   *— Mark 9:50*

Inever met a parent who wished ill will on their child, especially before their child broke. Some parents had not known where to find the right tools. Others actually discarded good tools and replaced them with poor ones. Occasionally, parents shunned helpful tools. All avoided the most basic tool—self-examination!

Connecting—heart to heart connecting with a child requires emotional availability. Emotional availability—the very heart of a relationship, requires self-examination.

Principle V: Remain Emotionally Available

...What man is there that is fearful and fainthearted? Let him go and return unto his house, lest his brethren's heart faint as well as his heart.   *— Deuteronomy 20:8*

There is a delicate balance between being emotionally available and becoming emotionally involved. When we are "emotionally involved" and become almost as emotional about another person's problem as they are, we actually become part of the problem, rather than part of the solution to the problem.

For example, my youngest son, Joshua brought a friend on his regular visitation weekend with me. On Saturday afternoon they were playing outside. Suddenly, Joshua's friend, Eric appeared. "Joshua needs you."

"Needs me, needs me for what?"

"He just wants you to come."

I followed Eric across the street to the cement culvert running behind the neighbor's house and found Joshua lying on the ground. I became so panicky seeing my son lying on the ground, I was barely able to listen to gather any information. Had it not been for twelve-year-old Eric, I doubt I would have responded in any appropriate fashion.

Eric tried to explain that they were skateboarding in the culvert, and he showed me the broom they had taken to sweep out pebbles and debris, to make a safe pathway for their skateboards. However, he said, there must have been one pebble they missed and Joshua had a big spill and apparently had broken his arm.

Finally, I looked at Joshua's arm. I believe it is at that time I began hyperventilating, and actually began to feel pain in my own arm, although Joshua kept insisting he was not in pain. To this day, I truthfully do not remember how I got the boys into the car and raced to a clinic that I remembered was nearby. The doctor on duty looked at Joshua and said, "Yep, looks like it's broken."

That was evident! What was wrong with this man? Of course it was broken! Why doesn't he do something?

The doctor then explained that this was only a clinic, but I could take Joshua to the hospital, which I, in my hysterics, had totally forgotten was right around the corner. I had wasted precious time! I should have gone to the hospital in the first place.

The doctor said, "He's going to be fine; but is there anything I can get you?" I realized that I must be green, evidencing significant emotional involvement with this broken arm thing, and muttered, "No, I just need to get him to the hospital."

While Joshua's arm was eventually repaired, it was evident that I did not respond very helpfully because, in fact, I had actually become a part of the problem! What if it had been a life-threatening incident?

I was very fortunate with my children, having had few medical crises. Thank goodness, because obviously, I became too emotionally involved to handle such situations well. I truly became a part of the problem, rather than a part of the solution to the problem. To ever become emotionally available in a medical crisis, I would need to do some serious self-examination about the reasons for my extremely unproductive emotionality in medical traumas.

Becoming overly emotionally involved is a significant roadblock to logic, let alone communication. We may work hard not to appear emotional, however the non-verbal signals are very difficult to hide. If we are touched by the trauma another is describing, we may grimace, frown, or even become teary-eyed. If we are repulsed by their problem, we might close our eyes or give evasive gestures with our hands. If we are disinterested we may look away, become easily distracted, even yawn. If we are angered by their problem we may turn red, clench our fists or even walk away in a huff. Our non-verbal communication speaks much louder than our words.

Remaining emotionally available requires the assurance that your own roaring lions are tamed, enabling you to remain sufficiently calm and objective to be able to pay complete attention to the matter at hand. That means, no receiving or making phone calls, no finger-nail grooming, no reading mail, no playing with the computer, no jotting down reminders of things you need to do, no watering plants, no checking your watch or looking out the window. These are all signs of distraction, clearly indicating discomfort with the topic and certainly indicating that you are not fully emotionally available.

Naturally, that is expected in the therapist's office! After all, the client is paying for the time. Of course, he deserves undivided attention. But, you are a parent, in your own home. Not only do you have your own issues to deal with, but there is washing to do, dinner to get ready, a lawn to mow, the boss on the phone, bills to pay, a car to repair, other children needing attention. How, with all of those personal issues and responsibilities, do you ignore those distractions to become emotionally available to the one needing your undivided attention at the moment?

You must take care of yourself.

There are three primary barricades interfering with being fully emotionally available when another person, even your own child, needs your attention.

Barricade 1: Untamed Roaring Lions

Who can understand his errors? Cleanse thou me from
secret faults.   — *Psalm 19:12*

To remain emotionally available you must resolve personal discomforts with uncomfortable issues. There is no easy way out of this. The only way to overcome uncomfortable issues is to face them, learn why they cause you so much discomfort, and then work to resolve them. Until your own discomfort is resolved, you cannot help others with their discomforts.

Barricade 2: Cluttered Lives

A time to get and a time to lose; a time to keep, and a time to cast away.   — *Ecclesiastes 3:6*

When we are distracted with commitments that consume our time, we are always watching the clock. It is very difficult, indeed impossible, to focus fully on unexpected crises when we are watching a clock. We must whittle down our obligations to assure that we have time available for the unexpected, but critical needs of our children.

There is no escaping it: there is a reason we bury ourselves in busyness. Certainly our activities are important—needed—even serving to change the world; but are *all* of those activities absolutely necessary or are some simply barriers, subconsciously but purposefully erected to prevent us from self-examination or intimacy?

The bottom line is that our lives are cluttered for a reason. We have some need for all that clutter or we would discard it. We must discover the reason for clutter, before we can discard it. That will require more self-examination.

Barricade 3: Unfulfilled Lives

Hope deferred maketh the heart sick, but when the desire cometh, it is a tree of life.   — *Proverbs 13:12*

When there are overwhelming voids in your life, it is difficult to give anyone your full attention. When we are struggling to fill our own needs, it is difficult to fuel the needs of others—even our own children. If you are not happy and fulfilled yourself, it is unlikely you can help your child become happy and fulfilled, either.

Taking care of yourself means you are fulfilled as an individual: Spiritually fulfilled; emotionally fulfilled; mentally fulfilled and physically fulfilled. There is no way to become a fulfilled person without self-examination. How can you discover the gaping holes, if you do not look for them? Sure, it's painful. But, remember the pain will long be forgotten by the time you are enjoying the joys of living a fulfilled life.

The likelihood of completely resolving roaring lions, totally un-cluttering schedules and being absolutely fulfilled simultaneously is nil. In life, there is bound to be at least some stress in one area or an-other. If we haven't overdrawn our bank account, we have a cold. If we don't have a cold, we had an argument with our boss. If we didn't argue with our boss, we lost our keys. If we haven't lost our keys...

How can you just drop all of these perceived challenges, road-blocks and threats, and focus? After all, if you don't find the keys, you'll be late to work and you already had an argument with the boss, you could lose your job if you're late, and besides you are coming down with a cold, you need to take something and have to call the doctor to call in a prescription and you need to get to the pharmacy before you get to work, where are the keys, you have got to go... and here stands your child, in tears!

You affectionately, but quickly pat him on the head, tell him ev-erything is going to be fine and to keep a stiff upper lip and trot off to school, as you return to your search for the car keys.

Consider for a moment his thoughts as he shuffles out the door, using his sleeve to wipe away the tears. Consider for a moment his thoughts as he sees his friends and joins them on the walk to school. Consider for a moment where he will go and who he will seek to comfort his buried pain; and you didn't even have time to find out the reason for the tears.

Certainly, all of those perceived challenges, roadblocks and threats that are distracting you are significant. However, to become emotionally available for your children, to truly make heart-to-heart connections, you must find a means to set all of them aside for the moment your child needs you. There is no easy way out, it will take self-examination. The more we understand ourselves, the easier it is to put our stressors on the back burner, at least for a moment, to focus on the needs at hand. It is not a simple task. It will require courage, and it will take practice.

Finding Time

*Whoso keepeth the commandment shall feel no evil thing:
and a wise man's heart discerneth both time and judgment.*   *— Ecclesiastes 8:5*

I know people who repeatedly tell me, "After this wedding, I'll
have time." "After this report is in, I'll have time." "After the kids
leave for college, I'll have time." "After the big meeting, I'll have
time." "After I get the house painted, I'll have time." "After the audit
is done, I'll have time." "After this… after that." It reminds me of all
of us who said, "After we have enough money, we'll start our family."
If we had waited for that to happen, there would be no children! It
never happens, if we don't make it happen.

If you want something badly enough you will find the time. I
know that from 20/20 hindsight.

*For years we packed up the car once or twice a year, loaded in one,
two, three, then four children and traveled 552 miles one direction to
visit my parents for a weekend. We arrived in the middle of the night
and spent the rest of the weekend shuttling between our bedrooms at
the house and my parents' restaurant. On a good visit, they could break
free for an hour to go out to dinner. We ate our breakfasts at their restaurant. They were so busy they did not have time to scramble an egg
at the house, in fact, there were no eggs at the house. We ate lunches
at the restaurant because it was their busiest time, they couldn't leave.
We ate dinners at their restaurant. Tomorrow would be their busiest
day, and they needed to prepare. Seven days a week, week in, week out.
Year in, year out, in thirty-three years, they left their business three
times to travel to our home. The minute they arrived, phone calls began*

back to the restaurant! It seemed apparent they really did not want to make time for a relationship with us.

Early in my career, I was talking to my sister on the phone, when she announced she was seeing a therapist. She said she had been depressed most of her life and was now on a medication that seemed to be helping. I never knew she was depressed. She moved several times over the next few years and having just moved again she had just started with a new therapist, when we were again talking by phone.

"You know what she asked me?" my sister queried. "She asked if my parents were alcoholics! I told her 'no!' They have a glass of wine now and then, but I've never known them to drink to any excess."

I agreed with her assessment.

Several weeks later, in another phone conversation, my sister announced with authority, "Our parents are addicts and we're children of addicts."

It was then that I learned that an addiction is an addiction, is an addiction.

As she spoke, it provided a great deal of insight into what we had been battling with, futility, all of our lives. Our parents were addicted—addicted to work—workaholics. The relationships in our family were no different than in any family with an addict. The main objective of the addiction is to avoid intimacy. It worked! There was no intimacy in our family. Had there been intimacy, I probably would have known my sister was depressed most of her life. Instead, we were like four separate robots, each going our own way under one roof. Then as adults, we went our separate ways, geographically.

I realized that I, too, had many of the hallmarks of the addictive parent; I had buried myself in work, I became extensively involved in community activities; I was fairly involved socially. I had less and less time for family. We were each drifting in separate directions. Was there any glue that could pull us back together? If there were, how would I find it?

In fact, damage had been done. My children had wandered off on their own roads to "Fun." By the time I decided to attempt to glue us back together, they liked their roads much more than any I had to offer. What could have been would never be. I had to accept that. I had to revise my view of "family." No white picket fences for us. To move ahead, I had to let that image go. It was a loss I had to resolve, before I *could move on. The idealized image itself only caused frustration and discouragement. We could still be a family, but it would look much different than the idealized picture that was never realized. It could still be a good family, even a great family, but it would not have a white picket fence. I had to start making time—when they had time.*

To make time for children—when they have time—it is helpful to prioritize exactly what is important to you. Then, when overwhelming responsibilities and challenges face you, simply go through your priority list and determine the number one priority, where your attention will be focused. Of course, you must believe your priorities are correct, or you will become fragmented again.

I was fortunate to have my priorities spelled out for me. I was sitting in one of those church services where you don't even know the pastor, but you suddenly realize he had a direct pipeline to your house, or at least to your heart. In fact, I was out of town, visiting a church with a friend, when I heard the pastor speak directly to me. "We don't have to struggle with our priorities. God actually set them down for us. All we have to do is follow them: First, God, then family, then work, then community and fun will follow."

That sounded very simple. It sounded logical, and on top of that, he said this was the road to "Fun"!

I knew I needed to prioritize my life. Therefore, if God is first (Genesis 1:1 "In the beginning God created the heaven and the earth." Matthew 6:33 "But seek ye first the kingdom of God, and his righteousness; and all these things shall be added unto you."), I must get involved in some Godly activities. I joined a women's Bible study. Most of the women were older and had spent years studying the Bible. I felt rather out of place with my very limited knowledge. However, they soon made me feel welcome and seemed to enjoy mentoring me.

Each time we met they shared experiences of prayers being answered. I was very impressed with their accounts of not leaving bed in the morning before they prayed. On one occasion I mustered the courage to sound very unfaithful by asking, "How do you pray the first thing in the morning? I'm so busy getting ready to leave, I don't have time to even think about praying until I'm in the car and well on my way to work?"

One elderly woman smiled and said, "Practice. Before your foot hits the floor, remember to thank God for waking you up that day."

Another added, "You can pray anytime—anywhere. God is there. He will hear you."

The others nodded in agreement and acknowledged that there had been a time when they too were so busy they forgot to pray, sometimes for days. Then one of the women said, "You know, God takes care of us twenty-four hours every day. When I realized I was too busy to give Him five minutes, I was ashamed."

I sat there, ashamed myself.

*The visual image of praying before I put my foot on the floor reminded me to practice. I have to admit that my feet sometimes walked quite a distance after hitting the floor, before I remembered. But, before long I could actually open my eyes and remember to thank God for another opportunity to make things right. And, if I followed my priority list, I had to find time for family (**Psalm 127:3-5 "Lo, children are an heritage of the Lord: and the fruit of the womb is his reward. As arrows are in the hand of a mighty man; so are children of the youth. Happy is the man that hath his quiver full of them; they shall not be ashamed, but they shall speak with the enemies in the gate."**), and I had to find that time when they had time for me.*

These were their rebellious teenage years and my youngest daughter, Melissa, began associating with a group of young people unlike any ever invading our home before. Their language was vulgar, and their manners rude. I was appalled that she would associate with these people, let alone bring them into our home. I finally did something I never thought I could do. I ordered them out of our home.

Melissa snapped back, "If they're leaving, I'm leaving with them."

I was horrified for her, but surprised myself when my words were, "If that's what you think is best for you Melissa, but always know that this is your home and where you belong. The door is always open for you."

She left. I slept very little. I prayed a lot. I was scared for her, because I knew the people she was with were probably deeply into criminal activities. I had no idea where she was. I had no way to contact her. It was summer, which even precluded my finding her at school. I questioned my reaction over and over again; I should have made her stay. I continued to pray.

One afternoon a week or so later Melissa popped in the house as though she had never been gone. I was so relieved to see her and more importantly, to see her alive. She told me she had only come to pick up some of her belongings, but was leaving again.

I asked how she was and told her I missed her. I reminded her that the door was always open.

It was two weeks later before she popped in the door again. She informed me curtly that she was only going to stay at the house until a girlfriend got her own apartment. "Then," she announced, "I'll be moving in with her."

I said, "Okay."

How many times I questioned my appearance of nonchalance at her dreadful, horrifying behavior, but something deep inside told me that to challenge her would send her running faster and farther than ever, in the wrong direction.

During the time she was gone, she had maintained her job as a checker at a local grocery store. She worked until after eleven at night and slept quite late in the mornings. I was working out of the house then, and was usually at home when she woke. She would immediately walk into the living room, turn on the television, lay down on the couch with her blanket and become immersed in watching a soap opera.

Not only did I find her silences uncomfortably deafening, I was irritated by the mournful sounds of the soap opera tragedies, day after day. We had enough problems; we certainly did not need to hear fabricated ones! But, I was so grateful to have her safely at home that I said nothing.

One day I was working at the table in the adjoining dining area, when Melissa began her television-couch-soap opera immersion routine. I was so irritated. I was trying to concentrate on a report I had to finish quickly for a court hearing and she had this annoying tragedy blasting in my ears.

As I was about to comment on the volume, what I heard come from my mouth was a comment about the behavior of the character on the soap opera. Melissa responded with a monosyllable. Encouraged that she responded at all, I asked how the character's problem grew to this level of depravity. Melissa seemed pleased to give me a brief history, which in soap opera lingo took quite some time to explain the convoluted, contrived details bringing the character to the current depths of her tragic life. My heavens, and, I thought we had problems!

It suddenly dawned on me that we were talking. Melissa and I were simply talking. No feelings. No judgments. We were simply having a small talk conversation about something very irrelevant. We were connecting on some level.

I made it a point from that day forward to be available, in the house and watching that soap opera every day from noon until one o'clock, with Melissa. Over time, our topics of conversation expanded to more relevant issues than the soap opera!

Melissa never moved out, until it was the appropriate time for her to move out. Interesting is the fact that Melissa never knew we were gluing back together through her soap opera. When many years later I told her what I remembered of that time, she said she did not remember it at all. But, she did remember the people she left with, and confirmed my suspicions that they were in trouble with the law.

While we never have had a white picket fence relationship, Melissa and I have a genuinely loving, caring and specially connected relationship. Most interesting is that she calls me often, long distance, to tell me to watch something on television. Often, we end up "watching" it—long distance—together! While I certainly prefer to connect with her in person, I love those special times of connection with her. To me those connections are actually better than any white picket fence could ever have been!

It may not always be convenient to stop what you are doing when your child is ready to connect. The means of connecting may not even be tasteful to you. However, if it is a connection you want, it will take connecting whenever and wherever your children will allow you to connect.

I remember standing endlessly in the blazing hot sun staring at greasy car engines, listening to lengthy alien-language explanations of the mechanical workings of a car, while Brent adeptly maneuvered our cars back into operation. I remember listening to exceptionally lengthy, detailed accounts of movies the children had seen, including musical interludes and lighting sequences. I especially recall the rock concert my children invited me to attend with them. I said, "absolutely not" and they should not go either! They insisted. I very begrudgingly gritted my teeth and went with them. The minute the lights went off, the entire audience lit up—marijuana cigarettes throughout the huge coliseum! The music and its message were almost spiritual!

I remember the girls urging me to go see a movie with them—"Dirty Dancing"! What kind of daughters would invite their mother to a movie about dirty dancing? I thought they were utterly disrespectful. They insisted I go, "You'll love it Mom, we promise." Very begrudgingly, I went. Not only did I love it, I've watched it time and again on reruns, and finally bought my own video of it! It was, in fact, the story of a piece of my own life! How did my children know me so well?

When my daughter and her friend secretly worked in exchange for time to surprise me with a hot air balloon ride, something I would never do of my own volition and certainly something I would never encourage my children to do, I gritted my teeth and climbed in! It remains a highlight of all my lifetime experiences!

Even if it takes gritting our teeth, if we let them, our children can broaden our horizons and greatly enrich our lives in ways we could never imagine. If we allow ourselves to trust them enough to share in their interests, we will learn much about our children. Isn't that how we form any relationship? We take a bit of a risk taking some time to try something new with someone we want to know better. We then have a new point of connection—something to talk about, something to share, something to remember together. Who better to take a risk with than our own children? With enough practice, tooth gritting lessens. We simply learn to keep our mouths closed until we know all the details.

For almost two years our family had been hearing tales of "Shaun," from Melissa. At that time, we hadn't met "Shaun," but it was evident that he had become an important person in Melissa's life. We heard tales about "Shaun's group," apparently a musical group with high aspirations. As a realistic person, my thoughts of course were, "Sure, Shaun and ten-trillion other aspiring kids." However, I kept my mouth closed.

When I heard "Shaun's group is going to China for a concert," I kept my mouth closed and wished them well.

When I heard "Shaun's group is going to be on the Jenny Jones show," it was really hard, but I kept my mouth closed and asked the name of the group. When I heard the name, "NAS-T," I bit my tongue to keep my mouth closed. One could just imagine what a group named "nasty" would sound like, but what I said was, "How exciting for them! What kind of music do they do?" Melissa assured me I'd like their music. While, I said, "I don't watch that show, but I'll surely tape it when Shaun is on!" what I thought was, "Okay. I'll get earplugs, close my eyes and tape the show."

Curious as I am, I didn't get earplugs and I didn't close my eyes. In fact, I happened to be home when the show was on—although I was taping, too. Here came "NAS-T" (Nubian Artists Striving Together). Now we don't all like the same kind of music, but let me tell you I was awestruck! I didn't like the music; I loved it! "Shaun's group" was super! Before they even ended their act, I was on the phone to Melissa. We rewound our tapes and watched a repeat performance—together. We critiqued the performance—together! We had a great deal of fun and a lot of laughs re-watching "Shaun's group" on national TV—together!

The moral of the story: It pays to keep one's mouth closed, until all the facts are in!

I learned a lot about my children by sometimes forcing myself to stop my self-absorption and withhold my judgment and just be still and listen. I learned more about their interests. I learned a great deal about their wonderful personalities. I learned of problems. I learned they might let me help them with their problems, if I would simply be there for them. Often, I learned that I had been criticizing and judging them for things I knew nothing about.

Always, I was rewarded far beyond the effort it took to tear myself away from self-absorption and busy-ness. The small connections could grow into deeper more intimate connections. Always, my reward for taking the time, even forcing myself to connect, has been a new opportunity to talk and share and grow closer to my children. As with prayer, practice has made making time to connect grow easier over the years.

It was very nice having my priorities mapped out for me. I don't know what my priorities might be now, if I had not been sitting in that church service. And, that pastor was right! "Fun" came, when I put my other priorities in order. I don't have to juggle work with family—family comes first. Therefore, I do not feel guilty when I am confronted with choosing family over work. I don't have to juggle my volunteer activities with my work, because work comes first. Therefore, I do not feel guilty when I must say "no." When I keep my priorities in order, I actually have fun doing almost everything I do! Of course, the interpretation of "fun" differs now, from when I was a teen and established "fun" as my *goal for life. "Fun" today means fulfillment. I don't have to go seeking fun; it comes to me when I choose to maintain my priorities.*

When we are overwhelmed—stressed by ever growing responsibilities, each of us sets priorities in his own way. I can share with you what works best for me—when I choose to use it! It may work for you, or it may give you some ideas about how you want to set your own priorities.

1) *I give my stress to God. He is much bigger than I am, and seems to handle my stress much better than I do. That is why I keep giving it back to Him. His solutions invariably work best.*

2) *Looking at all of my problems in one fell-swoop is overwhelming. When I am overwhelmed, I do nothing. So, I take the problems apart, piece-by-piece, deciding for myself which piece takes priority. By breaking the problem down into workable pieces, it does not seem to be so overwhelming.*

3) *It doesn't always work, but I strive to make people my first priority, with my own family being "1A;" friends being "1B;" co-workers "1C', etc. I endeavor to focus on the "people part" of the problem first. Very often, focusing on the people part spontaneously resolves the other areas of the problem.*

4) *Delegate, delegate, delegate. I try to find others with greater talents than mine to carry a share of the burden. This has an added benefit; it makes me look really good when I find people to help, who really do the job better than I could!*

Whether my method works for you or not, should you decide that setting priorities is a "must" for you, it will require some soul-searching—some self-examination. It is hardest to be objective about one's self. After all, it hurts to admit our flaws. Who willingly wants to inflict pain upon themselves? It is easiest to turn our back on ourselves and avoid dealing with areas needing change. We literally become habituated to avoiding our own shortcomings, because they are the most painful to face. No one enjoys admitting they made a mistake or have a flaw. Unfortunately, by avoiding our shortcomings, they consume us, becoming even bigger roaring lions.

For example, in my scheme of prioritizing, step number four, "delegating," took a great deal of time to accomplish. It was very difficult *admitting to myself that I could not be all things to all people at all times. Giving up my illusion of single-handedly controlling the world was not easy. In my frame of reference, asking for help was a sign of weakness. I had to change my whole way of thinking, to face my perceived weakness. Once I changed my perspective, I had to find a new way to respond to stress. I had to begin sharing the load; by delegating what I believed were my responsibilities. They were, after all, **my** responsibilities. I had to erase an entire memory bank of "should's" and "should not's" to permit myself to delegate.*

"You should be able to handle your own responsibilities."

"You should not have bitten off more than you could chew."

"You should be capable of resolving your own problems."

"You should not bother other people with your problems."

The list went on until one day I realized that it is supremely unrealistic and also supremely arrogant to think I could be everything to everyone all of the time. I think the realization of my pomposity was more repugnant to face than my failure to fulfill all that I had bitten off!

Self-examination is without a doubt, difficult. Pride is usually the culprit, holding us back from looking at our flaws. We know that if we look at ourselves, we will find characteristics we see developing in our children, and don't like! We also know, we may find things about ourselves that need to change. Few people welcome change. Change is awkward, uncomfortable, and even painful. It is not easy to push through the discomfort to make changes, even when we know change is vital to connecting with our children.

Seizing Opportunities To Connect

Walk while ye have the light, lest darkness come upon you; for he that walketh in darkness knoweth not wither he goeth.   — John 12:35

How do you know when you are looking at an opportunity to connect, or just another opening for more problems, more hassles, more arguments?

I could have gone to that concert and found the music appalling— even evil. I could have gone to the movie and found "dirty dancing." What if "NAS-T" had been "nasty"?

How do you know? What if…?

I cannot emphasize enough how important a prayer life is for a parent.

Not that long ago I had one of those insights I needed, and really might have easily found a lifetime ago. In my race through life, I must have run right past this one. It was always there. I was just too busy running to recognize it. Again, better late than never!

How often do we tell ourselves, "I should have listened to my instincts"? Or, "Why didn't I follow my hunches"? How many times have you said to yourself, "I should have known better… I just had this feeling"? Or, "I should have gone with my gut reaction"? Remember in school when the teacher said, "On multiple choice tests always go with your first reaction"? I believe I finally figured it out!

I believe the reason our instincts and hunches and gut reactions are best, is because they come straight from God. Then, lacking the faith to listen to that *"still small voice within,"* we muddle with it. *"Nah, that's too easy, there has to be a catch!"* Or, *"No, that's too much trouble!"* Or, *"It sounds right, but I think my way is just as good, and it's easier!"*

When we interrupt the initial thought, we interrupt a direct connection from God.

I do not purport to be a Bible scholar, however, when I read the following passage, it seemed to clarify for me the purpose of the manifestation of God we call the Holy Spirit. **"But, there is a spirit in man and the inspiration of the Almighty giveth them understanding."** —Job 23:8. That reminded me that when Jesus ascended to heaven and was no longer physically available to lead us, he left us his Spirit to lead us. (John 14:16-18) That Spirit, the Holy Spirit inside me, was my instinct—my gut reaction—my inspiration! That *"still small voice"* within that I refused to trust because I thought it was *"just me,"* was actually inspired by God!

Isn't it amazing how little we trust ourselves? Once we begin to respect that *"still small voice"* as a communication from God, it is much easier to trust.

I can't say I always listen, even now to that *"still small voice"* inside, but I do have a renewed respect for listening to my instincts, because I now believe they are God-given. So, when my children asked me to go to that rock concert, in all honesty my gut said, *"Now isn't this special having your children ask you to go with them? GO, see for yourself what goes on there!"* But I interrupted that response as unbefitting my parental role, when my own thoughts said, *"Are you crazy? They've got to be up to something, they want something, don't even let them go!"* I struggled awhile, before I remembered my first inclination—the response that while seemingly un-parental in a worldly context, was a direct connection with the Spirit of God inspiring me from within.

It was not my intent to sermonize here, but at the outset I said I wanted to share what worked and what did not work, for me. This worked, and has continued to work. It was that same Spirit that led me to *"dirty dancing,"* where I found a tiny piece of my life puzzle and had a new opportunity to connect with my children. It was that Spirit that caused me to soar high over the lush green hills and farms of Oregon in a brightly colored balloon and gave me a new connection with my daughter and a memory to cherish forever. It was that Spirit that let me begin a variety of wonderful connections with my children. How *could I not share a most wonderful parenting tool that may set things right for others?*

Having said that; let me tell you that no more than a week ago, my youngest son, Joshua informed me he is now taking scuba diving lessons. My first thought was, "How wonderful—how beautiful it must be under water with all the sea life! How proud I am of his adventurous spirit....," and I immediately said, "You be careful, that's very dangerous. I don't know if I like you doing that!"

Thankfully, God is still working on me, and when Joshua one day (hopefully) invites me to take the plunge myself, I pray I will be willing to listen to that "still small voice" that will probably tell me to join him in an adventure that can only strengthen the connection between us, and have the added benefit of enriching my own life!

What if the means of connecting does become a disaster? What if that concert had been purely "evil"? What if that movie had "dirty dancing"? What if NAS-T had been nasty?

By adjusting our attitude, even negative experiences can become positive connections. In fact, all that marijuana at the concert was just one of those connections. I did not just overlook the fact that my children were going to places surrounded by drugs and illegal activities. I found this experience an excellent opportunity to open the door for discussion.

I opened the door to this conversation by saying something as benign as possible. I quizzically remarked that I was amazed that with all the security at the concert, not one policeman made the least effort to address all the marijuana! This remark allowed the girls to tell me that it was futile for the security to try to be everywhere in the coliseum at one time. The conversation developed as we discussed issues related to legalizing marijuana and how "one little thing leads to another bigger thing," as well as how associating with people who break the law reflected on them, personally.

I could have stormed out of the concert dragging my children behind me, when I realized all of the illegal drugs around us, but I chose to stay for the uplifting experience of the music and the connection it would provide between my children and me, I chose to use the illegal drug use as an "opportunity" to open a door for mutual discussion on a very serious topic. I could have done the same if "Dirty Dancing" had been "dirty" or "NAS-T" had been nasty. The key is to seize the moment, take the best that it has to offer, and use it to build connections and deepen relationships.

How do you begin to make connections, especially when connections have been unplugged or even shattered?

You seize every opportunity; **EVERY** opportunity.

Anything and everything can become a connection between parents and children, from a television show to a car part, from the food you eat to hairstyles or the clothes you wear—even a plastic Easter egg.

It was just before Easter and I was preparing for my annual tradition of leaving a candy-filled plastic egg, with a Bible verse, on the pillow of every youth in the dorms I supervised at the youth facility. I had done this for several years. On the Friday evening before Easter, while everyone was out of the dorm eating in the dining hall, I raced through four dorms placing more than a hundred plastic eggs on pillows. I planned to do the same this year.

From within I heard, "Why don't you do something different this year? Some of these kids have found a plastic egg on their pillow for three years. Perhaps it would be more meaningful, if they received it differently."

The struggle was on. "It's easier this way. I don't have time to mess around with new ideas, it's almost Friday."

The voice within said, "Just thought it might be nice to do it differently."

From me, "What's the difference how they get the egg? They'll have their treat and be reminded someone cares about them."

From within, "It might just be nice to give them their egg personally, see their reaction. You've never seen their reaction."

My turn, "I don't need to see their reaction. They probably pop the candy in their mouth, toss out the scripture and stomp on the egg."

From within, "But, if you were right there, they might not react that way—if they do."

Finally, from me, "Okay, okay! I'll give them their eggs."

As the idea took hold, I decided that just handing them an egg was a bit too much like the benevolent benefactor bestowing the poor waif with a morsel. Besides, these kids liked games. I'd just make it a game, see their reactions and get on with my Easter weekend.

The Friday evening before Easter I loaded up a huge bucket with plastic eggs, each filled with candy and a Bible verse, and began my rounds of the four dorms. In three of the four dorms, several of the boys who had been there longest invited me to look in their personal areas. Even by the third dorm, I continued to be astounded, as each opened his cabinet and proudly showed me carefully stashed color-ful plastic eggs, each still containing a slip of paper with a Bible verse. Some of the boys read the verse out loud; some of them **QUOTED** *the verse for me!*

In the fourth dorm were younger boys. Only a few had been there since the previous Easter. They were very excited about the idea of the game. They could keep all the candy-filled eggs they could scoop out of the bucket with a large spoon. They lined up to take their turn. As in the other dorms, almost everyone scooped out one egg, a few two, balancing them carefully in the hollow of the spoon from the bucket on the floor to a full standing position. They marched off with their candy filled eggs, happy as could be! I marveled at how such a simple game could give these kids so much pleasure!

Up stepped Brian. At that time, he had only recently arrived on campus, with quite an infamous profile. His crime gained national attention. His picture, at age thirteen, was emblazoned on the front of a national tabloid. He was a quiet, polite, handsome thirteen-year old, with whom there had been little time for personal contact at this point.

Brian analyzed the bucket. He stared at the spoon. He looked again at the bucket, and slowly leaned over. Carefully, he moved the spoon to the bottom of the bucket, stopping briefly to look up at me. He smiled a huge winning grin, and slowly, ever so slowly righted himself to a stand-ing position, carrying three eggs on the spoon all the way to an upright position! Impossible, totally, impossible! Over one hundred boys, and not one had come up from the bucket with three eggs on the spoon!

Brian had just made history and given me an opportunity to make a connection with him, which has now lasted almost fourteen years! I mentioned "three eggs on a spoon," at our first formal counseling ses-sion and ultimately learned that indeed, this was a child of exceeding perfection. He had to be perfect or he was nothing—in his eyes. He had to get three eggs on a spoon or he felt like a failure—so he just did it! He always got three eggs on a spoon!

So, a couple of years ago when he wrote that he was graduating from college, in prison, I jokingly wrote back, "I'm sure cum laude." He responded in his next letter, "You know me—Mr. Three Eggs on a Spoon—summa cum laude!" He enclosed a copy of his diploma— summa cum laude.

Fortunately, he has decided he does not always need to come out of the bucket with three eggs on a spoon any more, and protests that he could never do it again! He realizes how that attitude caused immeasurable grief, the consequences of which he will live with for a lifetime.

From "three eggs on a spoon" we developed so many other connecting points, but that one has always remained our private special connection. When I see those bags of plastic eggs filling the aisles of the stores at Easter, I always stop, and take a few moments to think of "Mr. Three Eggs on a Spoon," very fondly.

If a plastic Easter egg can become a connection, anything can.

A Winning Combination

A merry heart doeth good like a medicine; but a broken spirit drieth the bones. — *Proverbs 17:22*

To reach the heart of your child it may be necessary to revise some traditional thinking about the role of "parent." Through the ages, the very word "parent" has traditionally evoked mental images of controlled austerity: a virtual act in maturity. Consequently, upon assuming the role of parent, formerly playful, fun-loving individuals suddenly donned newly acquired stern parent-faces. Perfecting the parent-face was apparently thought to be a prerequisite for achieving higher levels of authority. Parents came to be generally perceived as authoritarian oppressors, having as their sole purpose, the establishment of rules and regulations that they must enforce with strict, traditional consequences.

Traditions are good. I even suggest establishing some family traditions. Traditions are not the problem. "Acting" is the problem.

Feeling obliged to behave differently than the person you desire to be, is detrimental. It is detrimental to act as the dictator of your child, when deep in your heart you would prefer to be running a sack race with him. It is detrimental to act as the all-knowing authoritarian of your child, when in your heart of hearts you would rather be sharing cotton candy at the circus with him. It is detrimental to act as the militant guard of your child, when you'd rather be out in a field flying a kite with him. It is detrimental, even unhealthy, to act as if you are anything you aren't.

Pretending is great for children's imaginations, but it does little to build close, meaningful relationships with them. Pretending to be something you aren't, and don't even want to be, only adds discomfort and unnecessary stress to the already challenging job of "parent." Acting is a job, you already have one; you are the CEO of your own Parenting Business.

When your child was a baby, you probably thought nothing of rolling on the floor with him making coochey-coo noises, flinging him in the air like a bird or a plane, or playing rousing games of hide and seek with him. Then, when your child reached some random magical age, you abruptly hid your toys, permanently. Now, you stand on the sidelines in awe of the youth group leader who dons a pair of roller skates and races your child around the rink. But you—you are the parent! You must stand apart from the fun and put on that stern parent-face. You know the one: pursed lips; squinted eyes; set jaw; arm position selected with fists planted firmly on hips or arms crossed tightly over chest, based on current circumstances.

Where did that come from?

Why do we think we have to "act" to be parents? Why can't we be ourselves with our children? What happened to that child in all parents who played hopscotch, jumped rope, ran through sprinklers and took imaginary flight?

That child bought a myth. The myth many bought, upon becoming parents, was that to be a good parent, one must maintain control of their children.

Control and parenting have nothing to do with each other. Control is not parenting. Control is something one does with padlocks and chains, and even that is a temporary form of control. When you remove the chains, you are once again out of control! Regardless, you cannot control your child; he comes to you with his own unique spirit. Once he learns the one necessary all-powerful word, he is endowed with a free will all his own. I believe he learns this word even before his second year of life. What is the word? The word is, "No." Interesting! The very word that gives your child his autonomy is exactly the same word you used in your attempts to control him! You see, acting like a parent can backfire!

In truth, there is no correct parent-pose. Parents are simply older versions of the children they are raising. Who said parents must suppress that silly part of themselves, in order to fit the stuffy façade that mysteriously became sociologically expected of responsible parents? How does that parent-look make a parent responsible?

Responsible means "accountable." Responsible means "dependable." I've looked up the definition of "responsible," and nowhere was I able to find the word "austere." I even looked up the definition of "parent" and did not find the word "austere." In fact, responsible parents need to lighten up!

How can a parent be responsible and lighten up at the same time? After all, being accountable, responsible and dependable requires serious attention.

Ahh, yes! *But* a vital part of a parent's responsibility is to connect with his child in order to be able to lead that child to safe territory! To connect, especially to connect after connections have become frayed and broken, requires finding ways to connect that are appealing.

Take it from one who tried it, austerity does not work. In fact, the older your child grows, the funnier he thinks it looks. I think I learned that best during a testy encounter with one very tall, tough looking juvenile offender. Having unsuccessfully offered him several options for stepping back into conformation with specific rules and regulations, I assumed the stance. I believe I chose fists on hips for the arm position. I meant business!

His defiant expression suddenly softened, as his own angrily pursed lips turned into a broad grin. "Now miss, you're not going to try that mother-face on me, are you?" he chuckled, shaking his head in obvious disbelief.

I couldn't help but laugh myself—at myself! What must I have looked like? We stood staring at each other, until simultaneously bursting into laughter. We shared a good belly laugh for several minutes. Then, without another word from either of us, he turned to step back in the dinner line, strictly adhering to conformation with the rules and regulations expected. Our mutual laughter turned a very trying situation into a wonderful opportunity to connect, and taught me something important about the need to lighten up!

Disrespectful, you say? AHH BUT, as the responsible party, you are charged with finding *appealing* ways to make connections with your child. The parent-face, or anything remotely connected with it, is not appealing, but sharing a mutual laugh is. What could be more bonding for a parent and child than sharing a good belly laugh? What can cement an intimate connection between a parent and child more solidly than a spontaneous genuine bear hug? Can anything solidify appreciation and acceptance between a parent and a child more than a boisterous "high-five"? What can be more appealing to a parent-child relationship than a genuine expression of, "I love you."

So much has been learned about the healing factors of both laughter and physical touch that we now clearly know we will wither, and even die, without both. Actual scientific experiments and medical science has proven that! If we want to be responsible parents, why would we deny our children (or ourselves, for that matter) these critical, life-sustaining experiences?

Laughter is infectious. One person's glee can fill an entire auditorium with sparkling laughter. Unfortunately, other emotions are equally as infectious. One angry person can bring a jubilant crowd to its knees. One depressed person can crush a festive gathering.

Of course parenting is a most serious responsibility. There are many serious difficulties facing all parents: job difficulties; medical difficulties; marital difficulties; academic difficulties; friendship difficulties; behavior difficulties; financial difficulties; not to mention community difficulties; world peace difficulties; ozone layer difficulties, and the list grows. Isn't that enough to be serious about?

More important than acting serious about your parenting responsibilities, is making solid decisions about the emotions you want associated with your relationship with your children. Often parents act as dictators, because they fear losing control over their children. Unfortunately, dictators are generally angry and bitter people. Anger and bitterness beget anger and bitterness. Worse yet, parents acting like dictators, while suppressing their preference to laugh and play, risk becoming depressed people. Depression is an extremely pervasive emotion. Children in depressed families struggle against the misery of depressed feelings, often substituting them with feelings of anger and rage. Anger and rage erroneously look to children as if they will provide more power and control over their own lives.

Parents rarely recognize that acting as oppressors when they would rather be making mud pies, has made them depressed, so, they persist at the behavior. Subtly, depression drains energy. With barely enough energy to drag themselves from bed and go through the routine motions of daily life, depressed parents certainly do not have the energy to issue bear hugs or share belly laughs with their children. Lacking laughter and appropriate loving, physical touch, children are deprived of the very fundamentals that create the sparkle in a loving parent-child relationship. Craving comforting touch and uplifting laughter, children will seek it elsewhere, and often, in most inappropriate ways.

Finally, I know from 20/20 hindsight that it is very difficult, if not impossible, to parent with any degree of sanity, without exercising a strong sense of humor. The strongest indicator of emotional health is genuine laughter. When a person can laugh at himself, genuinely finding humor in his own mistakes, it is strong evidence of healthy self-assurance. Isn't that what we want for our children?

You can choose to **act** like a parent, or you can choose to **be** a parent. Being a parent does not mean being a bully, nor does it mean being a buddy or pal to your child. It means finding the resources to comfortably be yourself with your child. Then, if you feel like acting silly—act silly. If you feel like blowing bubbles—blow big ones! If you feel like running through the sprinkler—get really wet!

The bottom line is: Enjoy your children, have fun with them, and while you're having all this fun, remember that while parenting is the most serious business, maintaining a powerful sense of humor and being generous with loving touches creates the ultimate winning combination for a successful Parenting Business. Laugh together, hug each other and say "I Love You," a lot.

Your Parenting Business Start-up Kit

The following forms will assist in guiding the establishment of parameters for your own *Parenting Business*. Included in your Start-Up Kit are:

FORMS
1. Parenting Business FORESIGHT Appraisal Sheet
   a. Mission Statement
   b. Milestone Guidelines
2. Parenting Business Marketing Analysis & Strategies Worksheet I
3. Parenting Business Marketing Analysis & Strategies Worksheet II
   a. Marketing Analysis & Strategies
   b. Marketing & Sales Strategies
4. Parenting Business Procedural Strategies Worksheet
5. Parenting Business Management Structure Worksheet
6. Parenting Business Support, Training and Resource System Analysis Sheet

Note: You may want to hand copy the forms onto a full size sheet of lined paper or use the enlargement feature of a copy machine to create a reasonable size for you to fill in the information.

OUR PARENTING BUSINESS FORESIGHT APPRAISAL SHEET

Employ *FORESIGHT*! Take time to organize for a rewarding Parenting Business. Set your aim high, as you would for any business you might manage. Be creative! Personalize your business! Identify the strengths and weaknesses of your parenting business.

OUR PARENTING BUSINESS MISSION STATEMENT

Write a brief paragraph that motivates your Parenting Business Team to achieve your Parenting Business goals. Encourage all team members to participate in developing the Mission Statement. Use clear, positive language, (i.e. We WILL…) to respond to these three questions:

1. What is the ultimate purpose of your Parenting Business?

2. When, where and how will your purpose be accomplished?

3. What values and principles will guide your Parenting Business?

OUR PARENTING BUSINESS MILESTONE GUIDELINES

Establish milestones! Be specific. Set your long-term goal. Next, establish three short-term goals to help achieve your long-term goal. Setting milestones will help you identify where your business will be in 1, 5, 10 or more years.

Long term milestone (One sentence):

Short term milestones (One sentence each):
1.

2.

3.

OUR PARENTING BUSINESS MARKETING ANALYSIS & STRATEGIES I

1. Write one sentence identifying your Parenting Business "**Target Population.**" This one sentence will explain whom your business will serve, how they will benefit from your services and why they will want what you have to offer.

2. Identify the **Current Strengths** of your Parenting Business. People Strengths?

   Internal Resource Strengths?

   External Resource Strengths?

3. In one sentence describe how you will use these strengths to achieve the milestone(s) established in your Mission Statement.

4. Identify the **Current Weaknesses** of your Parenting Business.
   People Weaknesses?

   Internal Resource Weaknesses?

   External Resource Weaknesses?

5. Describe your specific plans to overcome these weaknesses?

OUR PARENTING BUSINESS MARKETING ANALYSIS & STRATEGIES II

This is very important to your marketing strategy! Who is the **COMPETITION?** Describe how your Parenting Business will respond to the **COMPETITION?**

List your competitors and describe how they might interfere with your marketing strategies.

COMPETITOR

INTERFERENCE

Describe the methods you will use to overcome competitive interference.

OUR PARENTING BUSINESS MARKETING & SALES STRATEGIES

How will you market your business? Describe how you will make your business attractive to its target population? Include the unique advantages your Parenting Business offers, especially over the competition.

All successful businesses have marketing slogans. Create your Parenting Business slogan! Write it here! Repeat it frequently for motivation! Put it to music and SING IT! Make it visible! Post it throughout your "business" location.

OUR PARENTING BUSINESS PROCEDURAL STRATEGIES

The Nuts & Bolts—how will you run your business on a daily basis? Who is responsible for what & when? Who leads? Who follows?

RESPONSIBILITY	NAME

* = Leader

What Strategic Relationships will be required to assure the success of your Parenting Business? What relationships *outside* the immediate family, including competitors, will be required to assure the success of your business? Note: SR stands for **Strategic Relationship.**

FAMILY SR's
i.e. grandparents; cousins, etc.

FRIEND/ASSOCIATE SR's

COMMUNITY SR's
i.e. neighbors; teacher (people)

i.e. school, church (institutions)

How will you assure that those **Strategic Relationships** support the goals and values you have established for your Parenting Business?

OUR PARENTING BUSINESS MANAGEMENT STRUCTURE

This is a good place for a Parenting Business Team Picture! Identify the members of your team... and if you plan to increase your "staff," be sure to leave room for the additions!

(photos here)

List the names of each team member (below). Include Strategic Relations (educators, clergy, etc.) you will recruit to help you achieve your milestones. Denote job titles, i.e. CEO, Pres., VP, Board Member, Consultant, etc! Briefly describe their responsibilities, as you would in a job description. Clearly distinguish leadership from assistants.

NAME	STAFF POSITION	RESPONSIBILITIES

Our Parenting Business Support, Training, and Resource System

Great managers provide great support, great training and great resources for their staff! Where will you find the needed *Support, Training, and Resources* to successfully guide your Parenting Business? Indicate the resources your staff needs to most effectively do their jobs. Specify your Emergency Plans, if the needed Support, Training, and Resources become drained or depleted. If resources are lacking, indicate how and where you will locate them. Note: **STR's** are *Support, Training,* and *Resources.*

Area of needed resources:

Currently available STR's:

Emergency STR's:

Back-up Plans:

CURRENTLY LACKING STR's AND THEIR WHEREABOUTS:

SPIRITUAL:

EMOTIONAL:

MENTAL:

PHYSICAL:

FISCAL:

OTHER NEEDED RESOURCES:

Index

O

opportunity 15

P

physically 14
pray
  prayers 19, 34, 35, 36, 37, 39, 211
prison 16, 23, 24, 34, 53, 103, 105,
    122, 224
psychology 15

R

relationship
  relationships 19, 20, 30, 36, 55,
    72, 86, 101, 117, 145, 147, 150,
    165, 177, 180, 199, 210, 222,
    226, 235
revenge 23, 24
role model
  role models 19, 29, 55, 56, 108,
    179, 181

S

searching 16, 102, 115, 158, 173, 217
self-loathing 23
Social Worker
  social workers 15, 16, 63, 64, 77,
    117, 125
society 19, 20, 21, 27, 29, 30, 55, 147,
    164, 168, 177, 178

T

20/20 hindsight 7, 17, 25, 33, 43, 44,
    49, 122, 137, 149, 150, 185, 193,
    195, 209, 229
The Powers That Be 28, 29, 30
tolerance 14
transition 20

U

understanding 16, 99, 101, 154, 158,
    172, 181, 220

V

violence 21, 30, 101, 106, 113, 169,
    188, 199

About The Author

Carolyn Esparza, MSW/LPC has over twenty-five years experience in counseling with individuals, youth and families. As Director of Trouble Bubble SOLUTIONS, Ms. Esparza facilitates workshops and seminars on a variety of parenting issuses. She also serves as a consultant to agencies and organizations on mental health and substance abuse treatment and invervention. For further information please visit her website at *www.TroubleBubbleSolutions.com* or email Ms. Esparza at *info@TroubleBubbleSolutions.com*.

Notes

Notes

Notes

Notes

Notes

Notes

Notes

Notes

Notes

I f you enjoyed this book and would like to pass one on to someone else, please check with your local bookstore, online bookseller, or use this form:

Name_____

Address _____

City _____ State_____ Zip_____

Please send me:

_____ copies of *The Parent Business* at $14.99 $ _____

California residents please add sales tax $ _____

Shipping*: $4.00 for the first copy and $2.00
for each additional copy $ _____

Total enclosed $ _____

Send order to:

Tsaba House
2252 12th Street
Reedley, CA 93654

or visit our website at www.TsabaHouse.com
or call (toll free) 1-866-TSABA-HS (1-866-872-2247)

For more than 5 copies, please contact the publisher for multiple copy rates.

*International shipping costs extra. If shipping to a destination outside the United States, please contact the publisher for rates to your location.